GREEK MYTHS & LEGENDS

Cheryl Evans and Anne Millard

With illustrations by Rodney Matthews

CONTENTS

2 Before you start

4 Map of Ancient Greece

5 Religion

6 Greek myths and history

8 The Creation

10 What the world was like

11 Demeter, Persephone and Pluto

12 Aphrodite, goddess of love

14 The goddess Athene

16 Apollo and Artemis

18 Dionysus and Hermes

20 Prometheus and mankind

22 Zeus's lovers

24 Perseus

25 Wicked Women

26 Evil men

28 Fate and three heroes

30 Love stories

32 Jason and the golden fleece

34 Theseus

37 Heracles

40 Paris, Helen and Troy

42 The Trojan War

44 After the Trojan War

46 The adventures of Odysseus

48 More heroes

50 Who's Who in the Greek Myths

63 Index

Designed by Kim Blundell

Additional illustrations by Nick Harris, Joe McEwan, Chris Lyon, Mark Duffin and Jan Nesbitt.

Cover design by Katrina Fearn

Consultant checker Penny McCarthy

BEFORE YOU START

Before you start reading this book, you may find it useful to know what to expect from it. You can find out in About this book, below. There are also some notes on what myths and legends are, and information which should help to understand the myths and the people who invented them.

About this book

This book is an introduction to the most famous gods, goddesses, heroes and monsters in Greek mythology. It does not simply set out to re-tell the stories in summary form, but provides a fascinating background to Greek history, the myths as religion, how the Ancient Greeks saw the world and, above all, detailed character-information in the Who's Who (see right).

The map on page 4 allows you to follow the adventures and marks most of the places mentioned in the myths.

The main gods and goddesses are introduced on pages 12-21. Their birth, personality, best-known exploits and the places and things associated with them are all included.

There are lots of stories concerning humans whose lives were affected by the gods on pages 22-49. They range from love stories to violent battles. There is only room to tell them briefly here, but the main authors used as sources are given in the box on page 3, so you can look up their work as a start to finding out more about the myths.

Who's Who in Greek mythology

A special feature of the book is the Who's Who on pages 50-63. In it you can look up all the gods, demi-gods, heroes and monsters that appear in the book, plus others that you may come across elsewhere, though there are more that there has not been room to include.

Every name that appears in bold type (this happens the first time it occurs on a page) has a Who's Who entry. Here you can find out about its family, career, supernatural attributes and distinguishing features. It can also be used to inspire fantasy-gamers.

What is a myth?

It is difficult to define exactly what a myth is. It is generally described as a story which is the product of the imagination. However, myths were obviously more than just folk tales to the Ancient Greeks (see Religion, page 5).

Some of them seem to be attempts to explain things that would nowadays be described scientifically, such as how the world began. Ancient people had no scientific knowledge so used their imaginations to fill the gap.

Others seem to be elaborations of historical events in which human kings or heroes became like gods and did things no person could really do. This type of story is often called a legend.

Others do not fit in either of these categories and at this distance of time it is impossible to know why such gods and myths were invented and worshipped.

Combining gods

The myths evolved over many centuries. During this time, there were wars and invasions in the area that was Ancient Greece (see map on page 4).

Conquerors and settlers brought their own gods with them, which sometimes took over from, or merged with a similar deity that already existed in Greece. This gave rise to different versions of the stories about the gods and conflicting reports of their parents or birth-place.

In this book, the best-known versions have been used, which does not mean they are more correct than another.

Strange behaviour

The gods did many strange things in the myths, which the Greeks accepted in supernatural beings, although ordinary people would not have been allowed to do them. For instance, gods often married very close members of their family, such as a sister or mother. They also tended to grow up instantly and were able to do miraculous things straight away.

Some of the things humans do seem odd, too. Exposing unwanted babies to die features in many myths, for example, and was not a crime to the Ancient Greeks.

Costume note

Throughout the book, characters are shown in costumes from Classical Greece (see page 7). This style is familiar as many works of art illustrating the myths survive from this period. It does not mean that earlier people imagined the gods like this – they probably saw them in clothes from their own period.

Greek authors

Homer (about 750-700BC) The Iliad, The Odyssey.
Hesiod (about 700BC) Theogony
Bacchylides (fifth century BC) Poems.
Pindar (518-438BC) Poems
Aeschylus (525-426BC) Plays, including the Oresteia trilogy, Prometheus Bound.
Sophocles (497-405BC) Plays including Antigone, King Oedipus, Electra, Ajax.
Euripides (485-406BC) Plays, including The Bacchae, Medea, Hippolytus.

How to pronounce Greek words

Many Greek names are long and look very hard to pronounce. A pronunciation guide to each name is given in the Who's Who entries at the back of the book, but here are some general rules for pronouncing Greek words which should help you as you read through:

ae is "ee" as in Daedalus (deed-a-luss)

c is "s" when followed by an e, i or y as in Circe (sir-see), Cerberus (sir-burr-us) or Cyrene (sire-ee-nee)

c is "k" when followed by an a, u or o as in Callisto (kal-ist-toe), Curetes (kyoor-ee-teez) or Coronis (kor-on-iss)

ch is "k" as in Charon (ka-ron)

e at the end of a name is pronounced ee as in Aphrodite (aff-ro-die-tee)

es at the end of a name is "eez" as in Heracles (hair-a-kleez)

eu is "yoo", as in Zeus (zyooss)

oe is "ee" as in Oedipus (ee-dip-puss)

ph is "f" as in Hephaestos (heff-eest-oss)

3

MAP OF ANCIENT GREECE

THRACE

MACEDONIA

Mount Olympus

Hellespont

Aegean Sea

Troy
Mount Ida

Iolcus

THESSALY

LESBOS

SCYROS

Mount Parnassus

Delphi

EUBOEA

ITHACA

BOEOTIA

Aulis

Thebes

Athens

Mt. Erymanthos

ACHAEA
Stymphalos

Corinth

Marathon

Icarian Sea

Nemea

ATTICA

ICARIA

ARCADIA

Mycenae

Cape
Sounion

DELOS

Olympia

Argos

SERIPHOS

Lerna

NAXOS

Sparta

CYTHERA

Knossos

CRETE

This map shows the lands that
we now call Greece and Turkey.

What is on the map

At the time when the myths were written
down, the area was not united into these
countries, but consisted of many small states.
The most important of these are shown in
capital letters on the map, as well as the major
towns and physical features, such as
4   mountains, that appear in the myths.

You may find it helpful to refer to this map
when you are reading the stories in this book.

RELIGION

The stories told in the Greek myths formed part of the religion of Ancient Greece. They illustrated the nature of the gods and taught what pleased or angered them, but did not set out religious rules or ideals like the Bible or the Koran.

What the gods were like

This pottery drawing shows the King and Queen of the gods in their home on Mount Olympus.

The Greeks thought of their gods as being rather like themselves. They were human-shaped; got married and had children; made friends and enemies and even had human failings, like jealousy and bad-temper, which made them behave badly sometimes.

Religion and everyday life

Religion was a part of everyday life to the Greeks. They often said a quick prayer before doing something, hoping it would bring them success. Each god was responsible for some aspect of life and people worshipped the ones they found relevant. **Pan** was the god of shepherds, for example.

Temples

These are remains of the temple of Poseidon, the god of the Ocean, at Cape Sounion.

Many magnificent temples were built to the gods. Some of them have survived and you can visit them today. Priests or priestesses looked after the temples and carried out religious ceremonies. People also had shrines in their homes, where daily prayers and private ceremonies were carried out by members of the family.

This is the Temple of Apollo at Delphi.

Oracles

The Greeks believed the gods spoke to ordinary people through priests or priestesses. These messages were called **Oracles**. The most famous Oracles were spoken at Delphi (see map on page 4). It was here that **Apollo**, the sun god, killed the **Python**, a giant serpent (see page 16). A huge temple was built in his honour. The priestess, or **Pythoness**, would go into a trance then people asked her advice, believing they would hear the opinion of Apollo through her.

Festivals and drama

This is a Greek comic actor.

The Greeks had special feast days for the gods when there were processions and sacrifices. Plays were performed telling the gods' lives. Much of what we now know about Greek myths comes from these plays by **Euripides, Aeschylus, Sophocles** and others, who were writing in Classical times.

Mystery cults

This pottery picture shows a secret ceremony to Dionysus, the god of wine.

These were groups who worshipped a particular deity in secret ceremonies. Members had to pass tests before they were accepted. The cults kept their secrets so well that nobody today knows exactly what they believed.

GREEK MYTHS AND HISTORY

Greek history can be traced back over 40,000 years. No-one knows when the myths were first invented. Many come from a time before writing and were passed on by word of mouth. It is probably the spoken tradition that helped them survive upheavals when writing was destroyed or forgotten.

The changing myths

Conquerors and peaceful settlers brought their own beliefs into Greece where they were adopted or combined with the myths and gods that already existed, so they changed and developed over the centuries. They probably changed less once they were written down, but different versions of many myths survive.

Below, you can read about the main periods in Ancient Greek history and what we know about the myths at the time.

Before 6000 BC: Hunter-gatherers

The area now known as Greece was inhabited at this time by wandering tribes, hunting and living off what grew on the land. We do not know what gods they believed in.

This figure is from between 6000 and 5000 BC.

6000-2200 BC: Farmers

When farming skills were developed, people started to settle in small communities and learnt how to make pots, weave and work metal.

Clues to the religious beliefs of this early civilization are found in objects such as this marble figure, found at Sparta (see map on page 4), dating from this era. It is probably a fertility figure, as the richness of the earth for growing crops must have been very important to these farmers.

2200-1400 BC: The Minoans

This Cretan wall-painting shows bull-leaping.

Greek society advanced and developed until about 2200 BC when invaders from the north disrupted the process.

The island of Crete escaped invasion and a sophisticated civilization grew up, called Minoan after one of its kings, **Minos**. Many works of art survive, illustrating some aspects of religious life. Bulls often feature in Cretan myths and some of these were later adopted by the mainlanders into Mycenaean mythology (see below).

1600-1200 BC: The Mycenaeans

This is the Lion Gate in the great city of Mycenae, which was discovered and excavated by Heinrich Schliemann last century (see page 40).

Gradually, the mainland recovered and started to develop again. It borrowed many ideas from the Minoans, and finally became more powerful than Crete. This civilization is called Mycenaean, after its major city, Mycenae. The historical events that inspired legends about human heroes like **Jason** (see pages 32-33) took place during this period. The truth was exaggerated and embroidered to form the legends, but there is archaeological evidence for some of the events (see pages 34 and 40).

1200-700 BC: The Dark Ages

Between 1200 and 1050 BC the Mycenaean culture collapsed due to civil wars and more invasions from the north. The myths survived, passed on orally through the generations.

The poet **Homer** lived at the end of the Dark Ages. He is said to have composed two great works about the ancient legends, called the Iliad and the Odyssey. They were not written down until much later, but the stories were already 500 years old when Homer was alive.

Homer probably spoke his poems while playing the lyre. Greek schoolboys in later periods had to learn parts of his poetry by heart and every scholar could quote him.

This picture shows a poet performing his work.

700-500 BC: The Archaic Period

Between 700 and 500 BC Greece once again became rich in art, literature, science and commerce. Trade was established with many Mediterranean countries, a new form of writing was invented and coins were introduced for money. They experimented with government and social organizations but their religion was still based on the ancient myths and legends, as can be seen from their art.

This Archaic silver coin shows a picture of Zeus, the king of the gods (see page 9).

500-336 BC: The Classical Period

This frieze shows a scene with characters in draped Classical dress.

This is probably the best-known period of Ancient Greek history. We know a lot about how people lived at this time and our image of the Ancient Greeks is probably most influenced by Classical art and literature. People lived in city-states, and much sea-faring and trading went on.

Many plays based on the myths were written during the Classical Period, and it is often these versions that have come down to us.

336-31 BC: The Hellenistic Period

This era is called the Hellenistic Period, after **Hellen**, a legendary ancestor of the Greeks (see page 48). The empire of Alexander the Great came within this period, and Greek culture spread across the Near and Middle East after his death in 323 BC.

The decline of Greece

In the last century before the birth of Christ, the Roman Empire expanded and became more powerful than Greece. The Romans were greatly influenced by the Greeks, though. They had their own gods but did not have such a complex mythology. Gradually they linked the Greek stories to their own gods until both

This is a Roman statue of Mars (Greek Ares), the god of war.

mythologies were almost the same. The Roman names for gods and heroes adopted from Greece are given in the Who's Who on pages 50-63.

7

THE CREATION

The Ancient Greek religion tried to explain how the world began like this:

Chaos

Before anything existed there was a dark nothingness called Chaos. Gradually the shape of **Mother Earth** emerged from the emptiness and formed the world.

Mother Earth's children

Mother Earth produced a son, **Uranus**, who was the sky. They then had children together. Rain fell from the sky onto the Earth, making plants grow and animals appeared from the rivers and seas. Next, many strangely-shaped monsters and giants were born. Among these were three who each had only one huge eye in the middle of their forehead and were called **Cyclopes**, meaning "wheel-eyed". Uranus treated them cruelly and banished them to the Underworld.* Later, some human-shaped giants, called **Titans**, were born who became the first gods and goddesses.

Finally, Mother Earth gave birth to the **Golden Race** who lived in an age without trouble or wars. Sadly, they had no children so the race died, though their spirits lingered on Earth to protect and help people.

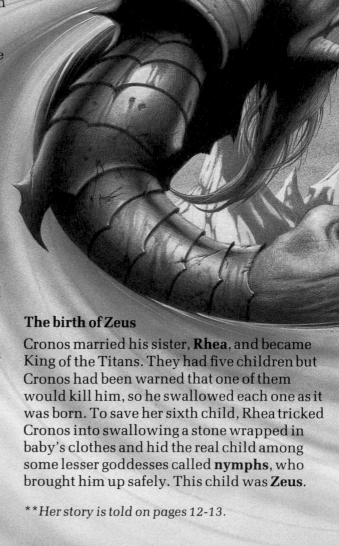

The revolt of the Titans

Mother Earth could not forgive Uranus for his treatment of her first children and encouraged the Titans, led by **Cronos**, to rebel. He attacked and overcame Uranus with a sickle and took power.

Three drops of Uranus's blood fell on the earth and formed the **Erinyes**, or **Furies**. These were spirits of revenge, with a dog's head and bats' wings. They hounded murderers, especially those who killed a relative.

Another drop fell in the sea, creating foam from which the goddess **Aphrodite** was born.**

The birth of Zeus

Cronos married his sister, **Rhea**, and became King of the Titans. They had five children but Cronos had been warned that one of them would kill him, so he swallowed each one as it was born. To save her sixth child, Rhea tricked Cronos into swallowing a stone wrapped in baby's clothes and hid the real child among some lesser goddesses called **nymphs**, who brought him up safely. This child was **Zeus**.

*See pages 10-11 for more about the Underworld.

**Her story is told on pages 12-13.

Zeus's revenge

When he grew up, Zeus returned home in disguise and slipped a potion into Cronos's drink, making him choke. The children he had swallowed were coughed out, whole and safe. There were his daughters, **Hestia**, **Demeter** and **Hera**, and sons, **Pluto** and **Poseidon**.

A fierce battle then took place. Zeus freed the Cyclopes who made thunderbolts for him to hurl. They also made a forked trident for Poseidon and a helmet that made its wearer invisible for Pluto. Most of the Titans and giants sided with Cronos.

After a terrible struggle the younger gods, or **New Gods**, were victorious. The Titans were banished and one of them, called **Atlas**, was made to hold up the heavens as punishment.

Zeus became ruler of the sky and king of all the gods. Poseidon was made king of the Ocean and Pluto of the Underworld.

WHAT THE WORLD WAS LIKE

The victorious gods divided the world amongst themselves. Here is what the Ancient Greeks believed their world was like.

Mount Olympus

Earth

River Styx

Ocean

Tartarus

Earth

Earth was where humans lived. In mythical times many weird and dangerous creatures were supposed to live there, too. Greek heroes often had to fight these monsters, as you will read later in this book.

The gods frequently visited the Earth. They sometimes made friends with humans or came in disguise, rewarding or punishing people according to how they treated the gods.

Sometimes they even fell in love with humans and had children with them. Many of the heroes of the Greek myths were born in this way and were half-human and half-god.

The Underworld

Zeus's brother, **Pluto**, ruled the Underworld, or Hades. Everyone went there when they died. There were three parts:

Most ordinary people wandered around the Asphodel Fields as "shades", which were shadowy versions of their earthly selves.

Tartarus was the place of punishment for really evil people. You can read about some of the tortures they suffered on pages 26-27.

Exceptionally good or heroic people were reserved a place in the Elysian Fields. This was a golden, blissful place of rest.

You could be sent back to Earth to live another life, but if you earned a place in the Elysian Fields three times you were allowed to go the the Isles of the Blessed, and never had to leave.

The Asphodel Fields. They were grey, shadowy and misty.

Olympus

The home of the gods was the peak of Mount Olympus. There was a real mountain in the north of Greece called Mount Olympus. It probably seemed very high and remote to most of the Ancient Greeks and therefore a likely place for the gods to live. Gradually, Olympus was associated less with the actual mountain and became more an imaginary place high above the Earth.

The gods lived here like a family. Zeus married his sister, **Hera**, and they ruled as king and queen. No-one but the gods could visit Olympus, except by special invitation.

Ocean

The Earth was thought to be surrounded by a stretch of water, called Ocean. This was Poseidon's kingdom. He controlled the winds and waves so he was very important to sailors, who made sacrifices to appease him. He was very powerful, but still had to obey Zeus.

Poseidon's wife was **Amphitrite**. She was a **nereid**, which was a sea-nymph.

The Styx

The Styx was the name of the river you had to cross to enter the Underworld (see below). You had to pay the boatman, **Charon**, one obol (an Ancient Greek coin) to ferry you across.

The Elysian Fields. This was a beautiful, golden place.

Demeter, Persephone and Pluto

This is the story of how **Persephone** became Pluto's wife and Queen of the Underworld.

Demeter was goddess of plants and harvests. She made everything grow and ripen. Her daughter, Persephone, was her companion and helper.

Pluto admired Persephone and decided he wanted her as his wife. He asked Zeus's permission but did not receive a firm answer as Zeus knew that Demeter would never agree, but did not wish to offend his brother by a refusal. One day, Pluto found Persephone alone and, saying to himself that Zeus had not forbidden him to marry her, seized her and carried her down to Hades.

When Demeter found her daughter had gone, she neglected the plants and trees to search for her. Without her care, the harvests failed and everything withered and died.

After a long search, she discovered that Persephone was Pluto's prisoner and pleaded with Zeus to make him release her. The gods agreed that Zeus should do something as humans were in danger of starving since no crops would grow.

Zeus said Persephone should be freed, as long as she had not tasted any of the food of the dead. In her misery she had not eaten at all, but just before her release Pluto tempted her to try a few pomegranate seeds from his garden.

"Since you have eaten from Pluto's garden," said Zeus to Persephone, "you must spend part of each year in Hades with him. The rest you may spend on Earth with your mother."

So every year, when Persephone was with Pluto, Demeter would mourn, plants died and it was winter. When Persephone returned, Demeter was happy again, things began to blossom and it was spring.

APHRODITE, GODDESS OF LOVE

The goddess **Aphrodite** was born in a most unusual way. When **Uranus** was defeated by the **New Gods** (page 8), one drop of blood from his wounds fell in the Ocean and caused the water to froth and foam. From the foam, the fully-grown figure of Aphrodite appeared. This was supposed to have happened near the island of Cythera*.

The loveliest goddess

Aphrodite was carried in a giant scallop shell to the shores of Cyprus where she was met by the **Seasons** in the form of beautiful girls who gave her clothes and jewels to wear. Doves and sparrows flocked around her and became her special birds.

Aphrodite was the goddess of love. She existed purely to be beautiful and adored and had no other duties, as most of the Immortals did. She had a magic girdle which made whoever wore it irresistibly attractive to other people. Perhaps it was because of this that **Adonis** (see right) and **Paris** (see page 40) preferred Aphrodite even to other goddesses.

Aphrodite's marriage

Zeus decided that Aphrodite should marry his son, **Hephaestos**, the smith-god. He was strong but coarse and born lame. He worked in the gods' forge making weapons and jewellery.
Aphrodite could have had her pick of men or gods, so she was not pleased with Zeus's choice and had many lovers.

Aphrodite and Ares

The most famous of Aphrodite's lovers among the gods was **Ares**, the god of war. Hephaestos did not like his wife's behaviour and decided to teach her a lesson. He forged a net of bronze links and hung it above her bed. When the lovers were next together, he dropped the net over them and caught them like fish. He called the other gods to come and see how ridiculous they looked. He forgave Aphrodite, though, as she was so beautiful that he could not be angry with her for long.

Hephaestos, the smith-god.

Ares, the god of war.

12

*See map on page 4.

Aphrodite and Adonis

Aphrodite and **Persephone** both fell in love with a handsome human, called **Adonis**. He preferred Aphrodite and Persephone was jealous. She told Ares that Aphrodite loved an ordinary man more than himself. Ares was furious and, turning himself into a boar, he chased Adonis and gored him to death. Where his blood fell the first anemones grew.

Adonis was sent to the Underworld, where Persephone was queen. Aphrodite begged Zeus to let Adonis come back to her and he granted a compromise: he must stay in the Underworld during the winter but in the summer he could visit the earth and be with Aphrodite.

The wrath of Aphrodite

Despite being goddess of love, Aphrodite could become angry, just like any other goddess.

A man called **Glaucus** insulted her and this is how she punished him: the night before he was due to take part in a chariot race she gave his horses water from her sacred well and fed them a magic herb. When the race started next day, the horses went mad and crashed the chariot, killing Glaucus. They then ate their former master.

Pygmalion's reward

Aphrodite rewarded faithful followers like **Pygmalion**. He was a sculptor who worshipped Aphrodite, but could not find a suitable wife. He decided to create a statue of his ideal woman. It was such a success that he fell in love with it, although he knew his love was hopeless. Aphrodite felt sorry for him and brought the statue to life. Overjoyed, Pygmalion named her **Galatea** and they were happily married.

Aphrodite's children

Aphrodite had several children. One of her sons was **Eros**. No-one knows for sure who his father was. He made people fall in love by piercing them with his golden arrows. He was mischievous and often made the most unsuitable matches.

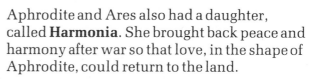

Aphrodite and Ares also had a daughter, called **Harmonia**. She brought back peace and harmony after war so that love, in the shape of Aphrodite, could return to the land.

Aphrodite's son by a human called **Anchises** became the hero **Aeneas** who was famous for his exploits in the Trojan War. You can find out what happened to him on page 44. **13**

THE GODDESS ATHENE

Athene was the virgin goddess of wisdom and war. She oversaw the safety of the state and was the most important goddess after **Hera**.

The birth of Athene

There are many different versions of Athene's birth, but this is the most frequent one:

Zeus fell in love with **Metis**, the **Titaness** of wisdom. She was expecting his baby when Zeus heard a prophecy that any child Metis had would be greater than its father. Zeus could not permit this, so he turned Metis into a fly and swallowed her. This was how Zeus gained his great wisdom.

Later, Zeus was walking by Lake Triton in Libya when he developed a terrible headache. He ordered **Hephaestos** to crack his skull open, which the smith-god did, as he knew he could not harm an Immortal. From the split appeared a female figure in full armour. Zeus introduced her as his daughter, Athene.

Goddess of wisdom and war

Athene inherited Metis's wisdom and preferred to settle disputes by reasoning. If forced to fight, though, she was invincible as goddess of war. She took care of Zeus's shield (the aegis) and other battle-gear.

The owl was her special bird and she was patroness of the olive crop and of the capital city of Greece (see story oppposite).

Pallas and Athene

When she was young, Athene had a great friend, **Pallas**. One day they were practising with their spears when Athene killed her friend by accident. To show her sorrow, she put her friend's name before her own and was afterwards often known as Pallas Athene.

The invention of the flute

Athene is said to have invented the flute. She first played it at a banquet of the gods and everyone seemed to like it, except **Hera** and **Aphrodite** who would not stop giggling. (There was always rivalry between these three goddesses – see page 41.)

Athene was puzzled until she glimpsed her reflection in a pool. She soon saw what they found funny, as to play the flute she had to puff her cheeks out, which looked silly. She cursed the flute and threw it away. It was later found by **Marsyas** (see page 17).

The naming of Athens

Athene and **Poseidon** quarrelled over the naming of the greatest town in Greece. At last they agreed that whoever gave the town the best gift should also name it.

Poseidon dug his trident into the rock on which the town stood and out gushed a stream, giving access to the sea so it could become rich and powerful through trade.

Athene created the olive tree as her gift. It provided food and oil for the inhabitants and made them rich through exports, so it was judged the better gift and the town was named Athens after her. A special shrine was built to Athene on the Acropolis (the hill above Athens). It was called the Parthenon, from the word *parthenos*, meaning "maiden", which was another of Athene's titles.

The weaving contest

Athene was also goddess of crafts. This story shows how proud she was of her weaving.

Princess **Arachne** was a skilled weaver. She even boasted that she was better than Athene so the goddess challenged her to a contest. They both wove the most beautiful work they could. When they had finished, Athene was infuriated to find that Arachne's really was equal to hers, and in a jealous rage she tore the girl's weaving up. Arachne was so frightened that she tried to hang herself. Athene was then ashamed and saved Arachne from death by turning her into a spider. Ever since then spiders have woven beautiful webs.

Athene's anger

Athene's short temper features in many of the myths about her. For instance, when a man called **Tiresias** accidentally came across Athene in her bath, she blinded him for daring to look at her. She made up for her hasty action by giving him the gift of seeing the future and he advised **Oedipus** (page 29) and **Odysseus** (pages 46-47).

Another time, a crow brought Athene some bad news. Until then crows had been white but in her fury, Athene turned the unlucky messenger black and they have been black ever since.

Medusa, daughter of the sea-god **Phorcys**, suffered too. She offended Athene, who turned her into a hideous monster. The story of Medusa and her sisters (the **Gorgons**) is told on page 24.

APOLLO AND ARTEMIS

Apollo and **Artemis** were twin children of **Zeus** and the **Titaness, Leto**. Artemis was goddess of the moon and hunting and protected wild animals. Apollo was the sun god and patron of the Arts. The raven was his special bird. Both Apollo and Artemis were associated with woodland.

The birth of Artemis and Apollo

Zeus tried to keep his affair with Leto a secret, but **Hera** was not fooled. She sent her giant snake, **Python**, after poor Leto, who ran until she collapsed. The **South Wind** then lifted her over to the island of Ortygia. Here, Artemis was born. She grew up instantly and helped Leto across to the island of Delos where she gave birth to Apollo.

Chariots of the gods

The Greeks believed the sun and moon were drawn across the sky in chariots. The sun was drawn by Apollo's golden horses and the moon by Artemis's silver stags.

The punishment of Niobe

Queen **Niobe** of Thebes boasted she was better than Leto as she had seven daughters and seven sons while Leto only had one of each. To punish her, Apollo and Artemis killed all except two of her children. Niobe mourned so bitterly that Zeus took pity on her and turned her to stone on Mount Sipylus so she could no longer feel her grief, but each year when melting snow ran off the mountain, the Greeks said it was Niobe's tears.

The Muses

Apollo tamed the nine **Muses**, wild goddesses who inspired artists, and became god of the Arts. He loved music and played the lyre.

Apollo's laurel wreath

Apollo pursued a **nymph** called **Daphne**, who did not want his attentions. She ran away, praying to **Mother Earth** to save her. Just as Apollo caught her, her prayers were answered and she was turned into a laurel tree. Apollo wore a wreath of laurel leaves in her memory.

The Oracle of Apollo

Apollo hunted down the Python that had chased his mother. He killed it at Delphi and a huge temple was built to him there. He gave his priestesses the gift of telling the future. Their prophecies, or **Oracles**, were famous throughout Greece.

The quarrel over Asclepius

Apollo's arrows brought plague and death but he also had healing powers, which he passed on to his son, **Asclepius**. He became a great doctor but went too far when he began to revive the dead. **Pluto** demanded he should be stopped, as the dead were his subjects. Zeus struck Asclepius down and Apollo killed the **Cyclopes**, in revenge. Zeus would have sent Apollo to Tartarus, but for Leto's pleading.

The music contest

The **satyr, Marsyas** (you can find out about satyrs on page 18), claimed to be a better musician than Apollo, so the god suggested a competition. Marsyas played a flute he had found, not knowing it was the one Athene had cursed (page 15). They played equally well until Apollo challenged Marsyas to play his instrument upside-down and sing at the same time. This was possible with a lyre but not with a flute, so Marsyas lost. The price of losing was death and Apollo killed Marsyas.

The death of Actaeon

Actaeon was a man caught spying on Artemis while she was bathing. She turned him into a stag and her hounds hunted and killed him.

Callisto, the nymph

Artemis and her nymphs loved hunting and swore to have nothing to do with men. **Callisto** broke her vow by falling in love with Zeus. In revenge, Hera turned her into a bear and Artemis set her hounds on the nymph. Zeus saved her before she was torn apart and placed her image in the stars as the Great Bear.

Artemis and Agamemnon

Artemis was angry with King **Agamemnon**. He was preparing to send an army against Troy. She sent contrary winds so he could not set sail and demanded the sacrifice of his daughter, **Iphigenia**, to appease her. Agamemnon was about to obey, when Artemis snatched the girl and put a deer in her place. Iphigenia was taken to safety and became a priestess of Artemis.

Selene and Endymion

The Titaness Selene drove the moon's chariot. She is often confused with Artemis. A man called Endymion loved her and wished he need do nothing but think about her. Zeus granted his wish and put him in an eternal sleep in which he dreamt of Selene and never grew old.

DIONYSUS AND HERMES

Zeus was an indulgent father, even when his children misbehaved. **Hermes** and **Dionysus** were both sons of his whose behaviour was not always god-like.

Dionysus

Dionysus's mother was a princess called **Semele**, daughter of King **Cadmus** of Thebes. Zeus visited her in disguise and her family did not believe her lover was a god. They persuaded Semele to ask Zeus to prove his identity by appearing as his real self. Zeus was reluctant, but eventually gave in. He appeared as a blazing figure, with thunder and lightening crackling around him. Semele was killed instantly, as no human can look at the glory of a god and survive.

Zeus was able to save the baby Semele was expecting, however, and this was Dionysus.

Hera heard about Zeus's new son and ordered the **Titans** to tear the baby apart. They obeyed, but the **Titaness Rhea** (Zeus's mother and Dionysus's grandmother) put him back together again and brought him back to life.

Silenus and the satyrs

Dionysus grew up curly-haired and red-lipped with mischievous, sparkling eyes. He was placed in the care of **Silenus**, who was one of the many lesser deities who lived on Earth and served the Olympian gods. He had a reputation as fun-loving and irresponsible and Dionysus grew up rather wild.

Silenus and his charge travelled the world, making merry. They were often accompanied by several strange creatures called **satyrs**. These looked like young men, but had horses' ears and tails. The satyrs knew the secret of making wine from grapes and Dionysus taught this skill to people wherever he went.

Dionysus and his band were not always welcome. Silenus was often drunk and the satyrs chased nymphs and girls when the wine made them amorous.

The cult of Dionysus

Dionysus was associated with nature and the woods. His symbol was the thyrsos, a stick entwined with ivy leaves, which he usually carried.

There was a mystery cult dedicated to worshipping Dionysus. They had initiation rites and secret ceremonies which only members of the sect could attend.

Many of his followers were women. They were called **Maenads**. They danced and drank in processions through the countryside and were notorious for wild behaviour. They danced themselves into a frenzy and sometimes chased and killed animals bare-handed.

Pentheus and the Maenads

Pentheus was King of Thebes. His mother, **Agave**, was a Maenad. The king disapproved, and when Dionysus came to Thebes, Pentheus threw him in prison. Dionysus pretended to submit, but he persuaded Pentheus to spy on the Maenads to see for himself how they behaved.

Pentheus followed the women's procession and watched them from a distance. At the height of their frenzy they spotted the intruder, grabbed him and tore him limb from limb. His own mother ripped off his head, not knowing what she was doing in her trance. This was Dionysus's revenge.

Hermes

Hermes was the son of Zeus and the Titaness **Maia**. He soon got a reputation for mischief. When he was only a few days old, he stole some cattle belonging to **Apollo**. He covered their hooves with bark so they would leave no tracks and hid them away.

The lyre

Hermes used a tortoise shell and the gut from one of Apollo's cows to make the instrument called a lyre.

Hermes is caught

Silenus and the satyrs helped Apollo search for his stolen cattle. They were drawn to the music that Hermes was playing on his lyre. When they saw the instrument and the cow-gut used for its strings, they knew they had found the thief. Apollo was furious and would not listen to any excuses. Eventually, Hermes stopped trying to appease him and simply played the lyre in the hope of calming him down. Apollo, as god of music, was charmed by the instrument and agreed to take the lyre in payment for his stolen cows. That is how Apollo came to own the lyre for which he became so famous.

Messenger of the gods

Zeus was amused by the exploits of Hermes, but could not allow them to continue. He decided Hermes must have a task to keep him out of trouble and made him the messenger of the gods and patron of travellers. Zeus gave him a winged helmet and sandals so he could travel faster.

Since he had bargained so well with Apollo, he became god of trade and treaties; and because of the incident with Apollo's cattle, thieves and liars prayed to him, hoping for sympathy.

Hermes is supposed to have helped invent the alphabet, boxing and gymnastics, too.

PROMETHEUS AND MANKIND

The **Titan, Prometheus**, was wise and thoughtful. His name means "forethought" which suited him well. He took the side of **Zeus** in the war against **Cronos** (page 8), and so was not banished like the other Titans when the **New Gods** came to power.

Making the first people

Prometheus is supposed to have created the human race. This is how it came about:

The first people on Earth were the **Golden Race** (see page 8). They disappeared as they had no children and Zeus replaced them with the **Silver Race**. Unfortunately, they started to do all sorts of evil things so Zeus imprisoned them in Tartarus.

Zeus was discouraged by this failure, and asked Prometheus to try his hand at making a race to live on Earth. The Titan had the idea of making mortals that looked like the gods so that gods and humans could understand each other better. This was the **Bronze Race**.

The trick

Prometheus was fond of the people he had created and helped them whenever he could.

There was a quarrel about which part of a sacrifice should be dedicated to Zeus. Prometheus found a way of settling it in mankind's favour. He divided a sacrificed bull into two bags. In one he put the bones with a few bits of nice meat on top. In the other he put the rest of the meat, covered with the unappetizing stomach. He invited Zeus to choose which bag he would like as his portion. Naturally, Zeus chose the one that looked nicest, although it was full of bones. From that time, the bones were always Zeus's share of a sacrifice, leaving most of the meat for the people to eat.

Zeus was furious when he discovered the trick, though he could not alter his choice. As punishment, he refused to let humans have fire, the gift he had intended for them, so they shivered in the dark and ate raw meat.

The gift of fire

Prometheus felt very sorry for mankind, and with the aid of **Athene**, his faithful pupil and friend, he stole some fire from Zeus's palace and showed people how to use it. They could then cook, make metal tools to cultivate the land and keep warm and this was how civilization began.

When Zeus found out what Prometheus had done, it was too late to take the fire away again but he punished Prometheus horribly.

Prometheus's punishment

Zeus had Prometheus bound to a rock with unbreakable chains and ordered an eagle to rip out his liver. Despite the pain, Prometheus could not die, as he was immortal. His liver was renewed every night and the torture started again every morning.

Many centuries later, Zeus allowed Prometheus to be rescued by **Heracles** (see page 39).

Pandora

Zeus punished mankind, too, for accepting Prometheus's gift. He asked Hephaestos to shape a woman in his forge. The King of the gods then breathed life into her and sent her to Prometheus's brother, **Epimetheus**. He gave her a jar, which he strictly forbade her to open, to take with her.*

Prometheus had warned his brother never to accept anything from Zeus, but Epimetheus welcomed the visitor and finally married her.

She was called **Pandora** and was very lovely, but very inquisitive. She longed to know what was in Zeus's jar and one day she could not resist peeping inside.

Out of it flew all the evils that plague the world—sickness, age, sin and death. As Pandora stared in horror at the empty jar, one last thing emerged. It was Hope, and it meant that people should never despair.

The flood

Zeus became more and more displeased with mankind. Once, when he visited Earth in disguise, a family tried to feed him human flesh. Zeus decided people had become so wicked that they did not deserve to live and sent a great flood to drown them.

Prometheus dared to interfere again and warned one Earthly king of the coming flood. This was his son, **Deucalion**.

Deucalion and his wife, **Pyrrha**, built a boat and survived the flood, which lasted nine days and nights. When the water subsided, the boat landed safely on Mount Parnassus (see map, page 4). Husband and wife climbed onto the land and sacrificed to Zeus in thanks.

Zeus had begun to regret destroying the whole human race, and was glad when he found these two had survived. He sent the **Titaness, Themis**, to help them. She told them to walk along, throwing stones over their shoulders without looking back. They did what she said, and all the stones thrown by Deucalion turned into men and those thrown by Pyrrha into women so the human race started again. These were the people of the Age of Heroes, which ended with the Trojan War (see pages 40-43).

*Pandora is often said to have had a box, but "jar" is a better translation of the Greek word.

ZEUS'S LOVERS

Although **Zeus** was married to **Hera**, he often fell in love with other beautiful women. Many of the children from these affairs became heroes or rulers. Hera sometimes tried to punish the women or their children, but Zeus protected them from the worst of her anger. Here are some of their stories.

Io

When Zeus fell in love with **Io**, he turned her into a white cow to hide her from his wife. Hera found out and tethered Io, leaving her hundred-eyed servant, **Argus**, on guard.

Zeus sent **Hermes** to soothe Argus to sleep by playing his lyre. One by one, Argus closed all his eyes. Hermes swiftly struck off his head and freed Io.

Hera was furious and sent a gadfly to sting her rival. The insect chased Io all the way to Egypt. Here, she became a woman again and a priestess of the Egyptian goddess, Isis.

Europa

Princess **Europa** of Tyre was on the beach when Zeus appeared, disguised as a white bull. She was afraid at first but the bull was so handsome and gentle that she soon started to play and garlanded him with flowers. She even got on his back to go for a ride.

At that moment, the bull plunged into the sea and carried her off to Crete, where she lived and had three sons with Zeus.

Later, Europa married the King of Crete who made her eldest son, **Minos**, his heir.*

Danae

King **Acrisius** was warned by an **Oracle** that he would be killed by his grandson. He locked his daughter, **Danae**, in a tower so she could never marry and have children.

He could not keep her from Zeus, though. He entered her prison as a shower of gold and Danae had his son, **Perseus**.**

Acrisius could not bear to kill them, despite the Oracle, so he set them adrift in a boat. Zeus guided the boat safely to the island of Seriphos.

22

*See page 34.

**You can read what became of Perseus on page 24.

Alcmene

Alcmene was already married when Zeus fell in love with her. She refused to betray her husband, so the god played a trick on her.

Zeus disguised himself as Alcmene's husband and went to her just when he was due back from war. She greeted Zeus fondly – and had a shock when her real husband arrived next day.

The couple guessed the truth, but could do nothing about it. Alcmene had Zeus's son and called him **Heracles**, ("Glory of Hera"), to appease Zeus's wife. This did not work, and Hera made Heracles's life extremely difficult, as you can read on pages 37-39.

Leda

Leda was Queen of Sparta, married to King **Tyndareus**. One day, she was bathing in a stream when a handsome swan swam up.

The swan was Zeus in disguise. He became Leda's lover and she produced a beautiful blue egg, from which were hatched four children, two belonging to Zeus and two to her husband.

Zeus's children were **Helen**, the most beautiful woman on Earth, for whom the Trojan War was fought (see pages 40-43), and the hero **Polydeuces**. The children of Tyndareus were **Clytemnestra** and **Castor**.

Thetis

Thetis was a **nereid**, a sea-goddess who could change shape at will. It was predicted that her son would be greater than its father. Zeus was in love with her but could not risk having such a son. He decided she must marry a mortal, **Peleus**, although he knew she would resist.

Peleus found Thetis on the seashore and seized her. She changed shape from woman to fire, water, lion, serpent and cuttlefish, but Peleus held on. His courage impressed Thetis and she agreed to marry him.

All the gods were invited to their wedding, except **Eris**, the goddess of spite. She got her revenge as you can see on page 41.

PERSEUS

Perseus and his mother, **Danae**, landed on the island of Seriphos and were looked after by King **Polydictes**.

Polydictes's challenge

Later, Polydictes tried to persuade Danae to marry him. She refused. He felt she might change her mind if her son went away, so he teased Perseus for preferring his mother's company to doing brave deeds like other young men. He said Perseus should prove his courage, by killing **Medusa** the **Gorgon**.

Perseus hunts Medusa

Medusa had been turned into a hideous monster by **Athene** (see page 15). She had snakes instead of hair and anyone who looked at her was turned to stone. She and her two sisters, also monsters, were called Gorgons.

As Athene had created Medusa, she decided to help Perseus kill her. She gave him a shining shield and told him to look only at Medusa's reflection, never directly at her. **Hermes** gave him a sickle and sent him to the **nymphs** in the Underworld to borrow **Pluto's** helmet of invisibility (see page 9). They also gave him a magic wallet and winged sandals.

Perseus sought Medusa out and attacked her with his magic weapons. He watched her in the polished shield, and managed to cut off her head, which he put in the magic wallet. He escaped on his winged sandals.

The freeing of Andromeda

Flying home, Perseus saw a beautiful princess chained to a rock and fell in love. This was **Andromeda**. Her parents had boasted she was lovelier than the **nereids** so **Poseidon** had flooded their land. To appease him, Andromeda was to be sacrificed to a sea-monster.

Perseus waited for the monster and killed it. He then freed Andromeda and married her.

When they returned to Seriphos, Polydictes was about to force Danae into marriage. Outraged, Perseus held up Medusa's head, the king looked at it and was turned to stone.

The Oracle is right again

One day, Perseus took part in some important Games. As he threw a discus it was caught by the wind and accidentally killed an old man. This proved to be **Acrisius**, his own grandfather, whom he had not seen since birth. The tragedy had been foretold by an **Oracle** (see page 5) and was unavoidable.

WICKED WOMEN

Wickedness, greed, pride and stupidity were all punished by the gods in appropriate ways. Amongst the characters whose behaviour offended the gods were several wicked women. The misdeeds of some of the most famous ones are told below.

Phaedra

Phaedra was the second wife of the hero, **Theseus** (see pages 34-36). She was jealous of **Hippolytus**, Theseus's son by his first wife. She made up a story that Hippolytus had attacked her. Theseus was appalled and asked **Poseidon** to punish his son.

As Hippolytus drove his chariot along the beach, Poseidon sent a huge wave which scared his horses, making them bolt. There was a terrific crash and Hippolytus was killed.

When Theseus learnt that Phaedra had lied, she hanged herself to escape his anger.

Danaus's daughters

Danaus and **Aegyptus** were grandsons of Poseidon. One had 50 sons and the other, 50 daughters. When their father died, the twins quarrelled over their inheritance. Aegyptus suggested that his sons should marry Danaus's daughters to make peace.

An **Oracle** warned Danaus and his daughters that Aegyptus planned to kill them, so they ran away. Aegyptus chased them, trapped them in the city of Argos and starved them into defeat.

So the marriages took place, but Danaus gave each daughter a huge, sharp hair-pin and told them to kill their husbands. All except one of them used the pins.

The murderesses survived, but when they died they went to Tartarus (page 10) where they were made to carry water from one place to another in leaking jars so they could never complete the task.

Ino

King **Athamas** had two children, **Phrixus** and **Helle**. Their mother was **Nephele** the cloud-woman (see page 26).

The king abandoned Nephele to marry **Ino**. Ino hated his children and plotted against them.

Ino lit a fire under the grain store, which dried the seed up so it would not grow. The crops failed and the people starved.

Athamas sent to the Oracle at Delphi to ask what to do. Ino bribed the messenger to say the Oracle's advice was to sacrifice his son.

Athamas sadly prepared to kill Phrixus, but **Hera** sent a golden ram to rescue him and Helle. She also made Athamas so angry that he forced Ino to jump off a cliff and drown.

The ram flew east, but as it crossed from Europe to Asia, Helle fell from its back and drowned. The sea was called the Hellespont (sea of Helle) after her. Phrixus landed in Colchis and sacrificed the ram to **Zeus** in thanks. Its fleece became the object of a great quest (see pages 32-33).

Scylla

The city of Megara and its king, **Nisus**, were under attack by King **Minos** of Crete. Nisus's daughter, **Scylla**, watched Minos from the city walls and fell in love with him.

Nisus had a magic lock of hair. As long as it was in his possession, his city was safe. Scylla stole the hair, slipped out of the city and gave it to Minos.

Minos won the battle and killed Nisus, but was so disgusted by Scylla's betrayal that he sailed without her. She swam after him, but her father's ghost swooped down on her as an eagle and she drowned.

EVIL MEN

The stories on this page are about men who angered the gods and were duly punished. It was not only humans that had to be taught a lesson, however.

Sometimes, Zeus had to punish gods for disobeying him or abusing their power.

Daedalus and Icarus

Daedalus was an inventor. He designed the maze for the **Minotaur** on Crete (see page 34). He offended King **Minos** who imprisoned him and his son, **Icarus**.

Daedalus planned an ingenious escape by making wings for them both out of feathers, wax and thread. The wings worked and they flew from the window of their prison.

Icarus was thrilled at flying like a bird. Despite his father's warnings not to get carried away, he flew higher and higher until he was so close to the sun that the wax melted and the wings broke apart. He fell into the sea and drowned near the island now called Icaria after him.

Ixion

Ixion was a murderer. He had killed his future father-in-law. Generously, **Zeus** was prepared to forgive him, but instead of being grateful, Ixion planned to carry off Zeus's wife, **Hera**.

Zeus could not believe he would really be that wicked, so he made a double of his wife out of clouds to see what would happen. To his dismay, Ixion pounced and carried the

cloud-woman, **Nephele**, away, proving how evil he was.

As punishment, Zeus ordered **Hermes** to tie Ixion to a wheel of fire, which he set rolling endlessly round the sky.

Phaethon

Phaethon was the son of the **Titan, Helios. Apollo** was god of the sun, but Helios was responsible for driving it across the sky in his chariot. Phaethon longed to have a go at the reins. He begged so hard that at last his father agreed to let him try.

At first Phaethon drove well, but then he began to show off. He rode so high that the Earth froze, then came so low that it scorched. Zeus was appalled and threw a thunderbolt at Phaethon, who fell from the chariot and was killed.

Sisyphus

Sisyphus was most unpleasant. He seduced his niece, took his brother's throne and betrayed Zeus's secrets. Zeus ordered **Pluto** to take him to Hades.

Sisyphus slyly asked Pluto to try on his chains to show how they worked. Sisyphus quickly secured them and took Pluto prisoner. This caused havoc, as the dead could not enter Hades without Pluto as guide.

Ares rescued Pluto and Sisyphus was sent to Tartarus, where he was made to roll a boulder up a steep hill. When he reached the top, the stone rolled back down. He tried again and again, but each time it was the same, so he could never finish his task.

Midas

To thank King **Midas** for looking after **Silenus, Dionysus** granted him a wish. The greedy king asked that everything he touched should turn to gold. He regretted it when even his daughter became a gold statue and food turned to gold when he tried to eat. He pleaded with Dionysus to undo the wish, which he did.

Later, Midas offended **Apollo** who gave him ass's ears. He hid the shameful ears under

his cap, but his barber discovered them. The barber was sworn to secrecy, but longed to tell someone. He dug a hole, spoke the secret into it, then filled it in, hoping it was safely buried. Some reeds grew on the spot and when they rustled in the wind, they whispered what was in the earth below and everyone knew how silly Midas was.

Tantalus

Tantalus was Zeus's friend and dined with the gods. He abused this honour by stealing ambrosia and nectar, the food and drink of the gods, and giving it to his friends on Earth. He then invited the gods to a banquet and decided to test for himself whether they were really all-knowing.

He killed and served up his own son, **Pelops**, at the feast, knowing that it was forbidden to eat human flesh. The gods knew at once what was on their plates and Zeus was so angry that he banished Tantalus to Tartarus (see page 10).

He was made to stand in a pool of water with fruit hanging just out of his reach; if he tried to eat or drink, the fruit and water moved away, so he was eternally tormented by hunger and thirst.

27

FATE AND THREE HEROES

The Ancient Greeks believed in Fate, which meant they thought their lives were predetermined by the gods. Even heroes were subjects of Fate, and had to suffer if they displeased the gods.

Bellerophon

Bellerophon was the grandson of **Sisyphus***. He was wrongly accused of trying to seduce the wife of King **Proteus** of Argos. Angrily, Proteus sent Bellerophon from his court with a letter to deliver to the King of Lycia.

The letter asked the King of Lycia to kill the person who brought it but he did not want to offend the **Furies** by murdering a guest. Instead, he asked Bellerophon to kill the beast called the **Chimaera** to pay for his hospitality. The Chimaera was a fire-breathing monster with the head of a lion, the body of a goat and a serpent's tail. The king was sure Bellerophon would fail and be killed.

Athene decided to help Bellerophon. She lent him her winged horse, **Pegasus**, and he flew over the Chimaera and plunged his spear down its throat.

Bellerophon then helped the king by flying above his enemies and pelting them with rocks. The king could not believe the hero deserved to die after this and they became friends. Bellerophon even married his daughter.

After a while Bellerophon became too proud. He tried to fly to Olympus on Pegasus. No human was allowed in the home of the gods without an invitation, so Bellerophon had to be punished. **Zeus** sent a fly that drove Pegasus wild. The hero was thrown from his back and landed in a thorn bush. He was blinded and lamed, ending his life homeless and alone.

*See page 27.

Orion

This is the star group called Scorpio.

Orion was **Poseidon's** son, a great hunter and a very handsome man.

He offended several of the Immortals. The goddess **Eos** was in love with him, but he abandoned her to hunt with **Artemis. Apollo** was on guard in case Orion insulted or hurt his sister, knowing how he had behaved with Eos.

Orion then angered **Mother Earth** by boasting that he could kill all the wild animals and monsters in the world, which were of course all Mother Earth's children.

She sent a giant scorpion to attack Orion. He fought bravely but soon realized that it could not be killed by mortal weapons. He dived into the sea to escape, hoping to reach the island of Delos, where Eos would protect him.

It was Artemis who was waiting for him on Delos, though. Apollo joined her and bet that she could not hit the small shape bobbing out at sea with her arrow. Apollo knew very well that this was Orion but Artemis accepted his challenge, shot accurately and killed him.

When she realized what she had done, she begged **Asclepius** (see page 17) to bring Orion back to life, but he was forbidden to do so by Zeus. So Artemis put the image of Orion among the stars, where he is forever chased across the sky by the scorpion (the star sign, Scorpio).

These are the stars called Orion.

Oedipus

Your Fate was unavoidable, however unfair it seemed, as in the case of **Oedipus**, son of King **Laius** and Queen **Jocasta** of Thebes.

An **Oracle** said Oedipus would kill his father and marry his mother, so Laius exposed him on a mountain to die so it could not come true.

A shepherd found the baby and took him to Corinth where the king and queen adopted him. He believed these were his real parents and when he heard the prophecy he ran away, hoping to avoid his fate.

On the road, Oedipus quarrelled with a man he met. Neither would step out of the other's way. There was a fight and Oedipus killed him. He did not know it, but the man was Laius, so part of the prophecy had come true.

Near Thebes, Oedipus met the **Sphinx**, a beast with a woman's head, lion's body, serpent's tail and eagle's wings. She asked passers-by a riddle:

"What goes on four legs in the morning, two at midday and three in the evening, and is weakest when it has most legs?"

She killed anyone who could not answer.* No-one had ever escaped until Oedipus answered correctly. The Sphinx flung herself over a cliff in humiliation.

The Thebans were delighted and made Oedipus king, as Laius was dead. He married the dead king's wife, Jocasta, and so unknowingly fulfilled the other half of the prophecy.

All went well for a while, but then a plague struck Thebes. The Oracle said the only cure was to avenge Laius's death. Oedipus cursed the murderer, not knowing it was himself.

The seer, **Tiresias** (page 15), revealed the truth and enquiries in Corinth confirmed it.

Jocasta hanged herself in shame and Oedipus blinded himself with her brooch pin. He left Thebes with his daughter, **Antigone**, and died near Athens. Theseus buried him honourably. **29**

*Answer in the Who's Who entry for the Sphinx, page 62.

LOVE STORIES

The Greek myths are full of love stories, both tragic and happy. Those who suffered for love were often rewarded by the gods, while the hard-hearted were taught a lesson.

Echo and Narcissus

The **nymph, Echo**, distracted **Hera** while **Zeus** chased mountain nymphs. As punishment, Hera condemned her never to make a comment of her own again. She could only repeat the last words that other people said.

Poor Echo fell in love with **Narcissus**. He was very handsome but also hard-hearted and vain. She followed him, helplessly repeating the ends of his phrases, until she faded away with sorrow, leaving only her voice.

Narcissus made many other lovers unhappy until **Artemis** decided to punish him. She showed him his own reflection in a pool and he fell in love with it. Realizing he would never love anyone else as well, he stabbed himself to death in despair. The flower called narcissus sprang up from his blood.

Oreithyia and Boreas

The serpent-tailed god of the north wind, **Boreas**, fell in love with a mortal named **Oreithyia**, an Athenian princess. She was dancing in a festival when he swooped down, carried her off and married her.

For his wife's sake Boreas always had a soft spot for Athens. Once, when the Persians were attacking by sea, he sent a storm which scattered their fleet and saved the city.

Phyllis

Phyllis and **Acamas** were devoted lovers. Acamas was the son of the hero, **Theseus**, and went off to fight in the Trojan Wars, which lasted for ten years (see pages 40-43).

Phyllis pined without him, and would have died, but Athene took pity on her and turned her into an almond tree.

When Acamas returned and heard what had happened, he kissed the trunk of the almond tree in sorrow. The tree burst into flower even though its leaves had not yet opened; ever since the almond has flowered before its leaves appear.

Orpheus and Eurydice

Orpheus was the best musician in Greece. When he returned from his travels with **Jason** (see pages 32-33) he married his beloved **Eurydice**. Soon after, she died of a snake-bite.

Orpheus went to the Underworld to beg **Pluto** to free her. He played such sweet music on his lyre that Pluto was charmed and agreed to let Eurydice go – if Orpheus could lead her from his kingdom without looking back.

Orpheus set off and Eurydice followed, but the temptation to turn round was too great. He looked too soon and lost her for good. Orpheus was so unhappy that he forgot to make sacrifices to **Dionysus** and the **Maenads** (see page 19) tore him apart. He was buried at the foot of Mount Olympus and birds were said to sing more sweetly there than anywhere else.

Orpheus joined Eurydice in Hades, and his lyre became the group of stars called Lyra.

Psyche

Psyche's parents boasted that their daughter was as lovely as **Aphrodite**. In revenge, the goddess told **Eros** to make Psyche fall in love with a monster. Psyche was taken to a remote mountain-side to await her Fate.

Eros went to obey Aphrodite, but grazed himself with his arrow and fell in love with Psyche. He took her to a beautiful palace and visited her there, making himself invisible, as she must never discover who he was.

Psyche's sisters visited her and were so jealous that they suggested her invisible lover must be a monster as predicted and that she ought to find out. One night, she shone a light on Eros while he slept. He and the palace vanished at once. Psyche was heart-broken. **Demeter** advised her to appeal to Aphrodite, who might then let Eros return.

Aphrodite tested Psyche to see if she was worthy of Eros. She asked her to separate a huge mixed pile of wheat and barley grains. An army of ants, sent by Eros, came along and did the job for her. Aphrodite next sent her to **Persephone** with a jar, saying it contained beauty cream. Psyche could not resist opening it, but it actually contained the Sleep of Death and Psyche was overcome.

Eros managed to revive her and Zeus decided to help. He soothed Aphrodite and made Psyche immortal so she could be with Eros.

JASON AND THE GOLDEN FLEECE

Jason was heir to the throne of Iolcus, but his uncle, **Pelias**, stole the crown when Jason was a baby. The deposed king and his son were banished, but when Jason grew up he came to claim his crown. Pelias said Jason could be his heir if he fetched the golden fleece from Colchis. The fleece came from the ram that **Hera** had sent to rescue **Phrixus** (see page 25). Pelias hoped Jason would never return.

The Argonauts

Jason had a great ship built and gathered a crew of heroes to accompany him. The ship was called Argo and its crew, the **Argonauts.**

King Phineus's advice

On the way, they visited King **Phineus** for his advice on the dangers ahead. He agreed to help if they could rid him of the **Harpies**. These were birds with a woman's head that screeched and snatched food, so their victims could not eat or rest. The heroes attacked the horrible birds, who clawed and slashed, but were driven out to sea at last.

Phineus knew how to get past the **Clashing Rocks**. They formed a lethal barrier at the entrance to the Straits of Bosphorous. They crashed shut if a ship tried to pass between them and crushed it.

"Send a bird through first," Phineus said, "to make the rocks crash shut. As they reopen, row between quickly before they shut again." The heroes did as he said and got through safely, though the bird lost a few tail-feathers.

Jason's test

At Colchis, Jason told King **Aeetes** their mission. He did not intend to let Jason take the fleece. He said that to prove himself Jason must harness two fire-breathing bulls, plough a field with them and plant some dragon's teeth. He was sure Jason would be killed, but the gods made his daughter, the witch **Medea**, fall in love with Jason and help him.

Medea

Medea gave Jason a potion to protect him from the bulls' breath while he ploughed. When he planted the dragon's teeth, armed soldiers sprang up and attacked. He took Medea's advice and threw a stone among them. One soldier thought another had hit him, fighting broke out and they all killed each other.

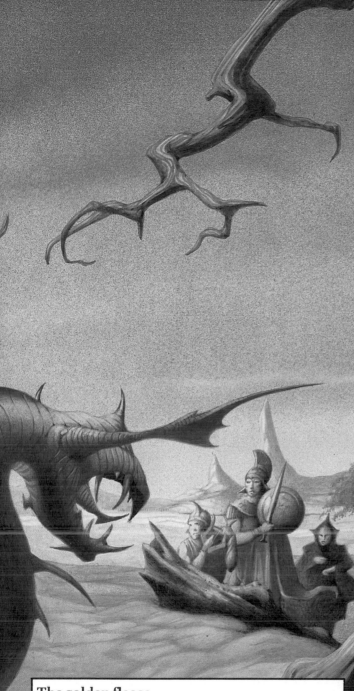

The journey home

Aeetes chased them and was catching up, so cruel Medea killed her half-brother. She threw his limbs overboard, knowing her father would stop to pick them up and stop the chase.

Some say they crossed Europe by river, emerging in the north and sailing past Britain, France and Spain on their way home. They met more dangers, such as the **sirens** on Capri. These were sea-nymphs who sang so beautifully that they lured sailors onto the jagged rocks. Orpheus played his lyre to drown their voices and they sailed safely by.

Approaching Crete, they were attacked by King **Minos's** bronze giant, **Talos**. He hurled rocks at strangers who came too near. Their weapons could not hurt him, but the heroes distracted him while Medea removed the pin which kept his life-force in. Talos then collapsed.

Medea's evil schemes

Back in Iolcus, Medea tricked Pelias's daughters into killing him. She said they could restore his youth by boiling him in a cauldron. The throne was then free for Jason, but the people were sickened by Medea's deeds and banished them both.

Medea was heiress to the throne of Corinth so they made their way there and Jason became king. He ruled well at first, but grew arrogant and broke his oath to Medea by planning to marry a princess, **Glaucis**.

Medea sent Glaucis a magic robe and crown as gifts. When she put them on, they burst into flames and killed her. Medea fled. Some say she killed her children first, others that the Corinthians slew them in revenge.

Jason's death

Jason lost the gods' favour and ended his life an outcast. He roamed until he came across the rotting hull of the Argo. Here, he sat down and was dreaming of the past when the prow fell and killed him. His death was a warning to anyone who broke his oath.

The golden fleece

Medea then told Jason how to deal with the dragon-serpent guarding the fleece. This monster had a dragon's head and serpent's body and was never known to sleep. On Medea's advice, Jason asked **Orpheus** to play a lullaby on his lyre until finally the beast closed its eyes. Jason grabbed the fleece and ran back to the Argo, taking Medea and her half-brother with him. Jason swore to marry Medea and be faithful to her.

THESEUS

Theseus was a popular Greek hero. His best-known adventure was on Crete, where he fought the **Minotaur** (see picture, opposite).

Before you read the story you may be interested to find out a bit about the Minoan culture on Crete (see box, below).

The truth behind the tale?

The story of Theseus and the Minotaur takes place on the island of Crete. Quite a lot is known about Crete at the time when this adventure is supposed to have taken place. The civilization of the time was called Minoan (see history on pages 6-7).

In 1894 the archaeologist, Sir Arthur Evans, arrived in Crete and began excavating. His workmen started to dig out the ruins of Knossos, the palace of King Minos, in 1900. Much remained of this huge, splendid building and many works of art were recovered. It is easy to imagine that the size and complexity of the palace gave rise to the idea of the maze, or Labyrinth, at Knossos where the Minotaur was imprisoned in the story of Theseus.

Bulls in Cretan mythology

The Mediterranean has always suffered from earthquakes. The Minoans of Ancient Crete may have been trying to explain these disturbances when they invented the story of a bull-monster that lived beneath the island. Its stamping and bellowing was said to make the ground tremble. The Minotaur was supposed to be descended from this underground bull. Bulls played an important part in Cretan mythology and stories like Theseus and the Minotaur were probably inspired by Cretan beliefs.

Theseus and the Minotaur

Theseus was brought up by his mother. No-one was sure who his father was as both **Poseidon** and King **Aegeus** of Athens had loved his mother. She hoped that Aegeus would make the boy his successor.

Aegeus's wife was the witch **Medea**, who had previously been married to **Jason** (see pages 32-33). When Theseus grew up and came to court, Medea recognized him through her magic powers. She did not want the king to discover his identity, since she wanted her own son by Aegeus to be the only heir to his throne.

Medea persuaded Aegeus that Theseus was a dangerous enemy and prepared a cup of poison which she gave him. As he was about to drink it, the king recognized the sword Theseus was wearing. He had given it to Theseus's mother as a gift for their son, if they should have one.

Theseus was welcomed and declared as successor to Aegeus. Medea escaped in her serpent-drawn chariot. Her evil plans had failed again.

Minos's victims

Several years before, King Minos's son had been killed in Athens. In compensation, Minos demanded that fourteen young Athenians should be sent to Crete every nine years to be fed to the Minotaur.

The Minotaur was a dreadful beast with the head and shoulders of a bull and the body of a man. It fed on human flesh and was kept in a maze called the Labyrinth, which had been designed by the craftsman, **Daedalus** (see page 49). No-one who entered the maze ever came out alive.

THESEUS AND THE MINOTAUR CONTINUED

When the time came for the next victims to go to Crete, Theseus said he would go as one of them and try to kill the Minotaur. The king was afraid for his son. He could hardly bear waiting for news, and asked the sailors who took Theseus to Crete to hoist white sails when they returned if all was well and Theseus was alive.

Minos's dare

Minos recognized Theseus among the Athenians and taunted him about who his father was. He dared Theseus to prove he was the son of Poseidon by retrieving a ring that he threw into the sea. Theseus dived after it, praying to Poseidon for help. The **nereids** found the ring for him and **Amphitrite** presented him with the crown worn by **Thetis** on her wedding day. He emerged from the water triumphant with Minos's ring and the crown.

Into the Labyrinth

Minos's daughter, **Ariadne**, fell in love with Theseus when she saw him among the victims. She offered to help him kill the Minotaur if he would marry her and he agreed. She gave him a magic ball of twine. He tied one end to the entrance of the maze, then followed as it unwound and led him into the centre of the Labyrinth where the Minotaur lurked.

Theseus's return

There was a terrible fight, but Theseus overcame the Minotaur at last and followed the path marked by the magic twine out of the Labyrinth, leading the other young Athenians, who had been saved from their Fate.

They escaped by boat and took Ariadne with them. On their way home they stopped at the island of Naxos. Here, while Ariadne was sleeping, ungrateful Theseus sailed off without her, forgetting that he owed his success to her and had promised to marry her. When she woke up alone and realized she had been abandoned, she cried to the gods for revenge.

The god, **Dionysus**, happened to be passing Naxos soon after. He saw Ariadne and fell in love with her. She became his wife and he soon granted her revenge by making Theseus so glad to be going home that he forgot to give the order to raise white sails and approached Athens with black sails on the mast. When Aegeus saw them, he believed his son must be dead, jumped into the sea and drowned himself in despair. The sea where this happened was called Aegean after him.

What became of Theseus

In these sad circumstances, Theseus became king of Athens in his father's place. He married **Hippolyte**, an **Amazon** queen. She later died fighting at Theseus's side in battle. Their son, **Hippolytus**, was killed through the wickedness of Theseus's jealous second wife, **Phaedra** (see page 25).

After these tragic deaths, Theseus became careless of his kingly duties and went adventuring again. He kidnapped the young **Helen** of Troy (see page 41), whose brothers had to raid Athens to rescue her. He also went to Tartarus with his friend, **Pirithous**, who planned to snatch **Persephone**. They were caught by the gods and put in chains of forgetfulness. Theseus was later rescued by **Heracles** but while he was away, his throne was taken from him.

Theseus settled on the island of Scyros, and died there, but his love for Athens outlasted his death. When the city was about to lose the battle of Marathon, his ghost appeared to inspire the troops and led them to victory. After that his body was brought home and buried with honours in Athens.

Amazons

The Amazons were a mythical race of warrior women from south-west Asia. They were very fierce and were not generally sympathetic to men. They were sometimes said to cut their right breast off so they could draw their bowstring more easily.

HERACLES

One of the Greeks' favourite heroes was **Heracles**. You may know him as Hercules, which is the Roman version of his name. He was exceptionally strong and brave, but **Hera** made his life extremely difficult as he reminded her of **Zeus's** infidelity (see page 23).

The baby Heracles

When Heracles was a baby, Hera sent two deadly serpents to his cradle to kill him. Heracles strangled them both, surprising everyone with his strength.

Hera's revenge

Heracles married **Megara**, had a family and became famous for his great courage. Hera was jealous of his happiness and drove him mad so that he killed his wife and children. When he recovered and saw what he had done he was horrified and asked the **Oracle** how he could make amends. He was told to offer himself as a slave to King **Eurystheus**.

Eurystheus set Heracles twelve "impossible" tasks. If he could do them all, he would get rid of his guilt and become an Immortal. They were called his Twelve Labours and are described below and over the page.

1. To kill the Nemean lion

This lion from Nemea had a hide so tough that no weapon could pierce it. Heracles had to strangle it with his bare hands. Afterwards, he wore the lion's skin as protection.

2. To destroy the Lernaean Hydra

In the swamps of Lerna lived the Hydra. It had a dog-like body and nine serpent's heads, which grew again each time they were cut off. Heracles had to strike off each head and seal the neck with a burning torch before he could kill it.

3. To capture the Cerynean hind alive

This deer had hooves of bronze, horns of gold and was sacred to **Artemis**. Catching it alive was even more difficult than killing it. Heracles stalked it for a whole year before being able to catch it in a net and carry it to **Eurystheus**.

4. To trap the Erymanthian boar

Heracles drove the enormous, fierce creature into a deep snowdrift and when it was trapped he tied it with chains.

5. To clean the Augean stables

The stables of King **Augeus** had not been cleaned for years and were piled high with dung. Heracles was told to clean them thoroughly in one day. Not even Heracles could have done it by himself. He succeeded, though, by diverting the course of a nearby river so that it swept through the stables and washed all the muck away.

6. To get rid of the Stymphalian birds

These were man-eating birds with bronze beaks, claws and wings. Heracles startled them with a great shout so that they flew up, then shot them with his arrows.

7. To capture the Cretan bull

This bull was father of the **Minotaur** (see page 34). It ran wild on Crete, causing great damage. Heracles managed to master the animal and take it back to Eurystheus by boat.

8. To round up the mares of Diomedes

These horses fed on human flesh and were extremely wild. Their master was called **Diomedes**. Heracles killed Diomedes first and fed him to the mares. When they were full they were relatively calm and he got them under control.

9. To fetch Hippolyte's girdle, or belt

Hippolyte was Queen of the **Amazons** (see page 36). She was quite happy to give Heracles her girdle, but **Hera** made the Amazons think he was hurting her, so they attacked and he had to fight their whole army to get the belt.

10. To fetch the cattle of Geryon

Gibraltar and Ceuta were said to be the remains of the Pillars of Heracles.

Spain

Gibraltar

Ceuta

Morocco

These cattle lived on an island in the far west, guarded by **Orthrus**, a two-headed dog, and the herdsman **Geryon** who had three bodies above the waist. Heracles killed them both and drove the cattle home. On his way west, he placed two pillars, one in Spain and one in Morocco, to guard the Mediterranean.

11. To fetch the golden apples of the Hesperides

The golden apples belonged to Hera. They were kept by the **Hesperides** who were the daughters of the **Titan, Atlas.**

Heracles did not know where the Hesperides kept the apples so he went to ask their father. Atlas had to support the weight of the heavens on his shoulders (see page 9), but he said that if Heracles would just take his place for a while, he would go and fetch the apples himself. Heracles agreed and Atlas set off.

Atlas returned with the apples, but had enjoyed his freedom so much that he refused to take his burden back. He said he would take the apples to Eurystheus himself. Heracles had to think quickly. He pretended to be willing to swap places with Atlas, but asked the Titan to take the weight for a moment so that he could settle it more comfortably. Atlas did so, and Heracles made his escape.

12. To bring Cerberus from Tartarus

Cerberus was a monstrous, three-headed dog who guarded the gates of the Underworld and prevented anyone leaving the land of the dead. **Pluto** gave Heracles permission to take Cerberus as long as he did not use any weapons. The hero had to drag the struggling animal all the way to the court of Eurystheus.

Other adventures

Heracles had many other adventures. On one journey he killed the eagle that tormented **Prometheus** and freed him (see pages 20-21). He sailed with the **Argonauts** (see pages 32-33) and also freed **Theseus** from his chains in the Underworld (see page 36). He still suffered fits of madness sent by Hera, until he was finally cured by the witch, **Medea**.

The death of Heracles

Heracles later married **Deianeira** and they had several children, but Hera finally caused his death. She tricked Deianeira into giving Heracles a magic robe. She told her the magic would keep Heracles faithful to her, but in fact it was poisoned. The shirt caused agony when he put it on and he could not remove it. He had a funeral pyre built and climbed on it to die and escape the pain. **Zeus** snatched his son from the fire and took him to Mount Olympus, where he became an Immortal.

PARIS, HELEN AND TROY

The 'real' Troy

According to **Homer**, the great city of Troy stood in a commanding position overlooking the Hellespont. At the end of the nineteenth century, a German businessman called Heinrich Schliemann, who passionately believed that Homer's poem was a true account of an actual event, set out to prove that Troy had actually existed. Following clues in Homer, he explored the area and, in 1870, found the ruins of several cities, one on top of the other, just where Homer had said. Experts disagree about which layer of ruins might be Homer's Troy, but it seems clear that it was a real place.

This map shows the position of Troy and the other main places mentioned in the story of the Trojan War.

Actual wars?

The story of the Trojan Wars probably arose out of an actual war between the Greeks and Trojans. It seems likely that the Hittites, who had an established empire in what is now Turkey, encouraged Troy to thwart the ambitious Greeks' attempts to expand their trade and influence into the Black Sea area.

Greece and Troy were traditional rivals, according to legend. Their quarrelling finally led to a long and bitter war. It started with the love story of **Paris** and **Helen**, which you can read about below.

Paris

Paris was the son of King **Priam** and Queen **Hecuba** of Troy. At his birth it was predicted that he would cause the downfall of Troy so he was left on a hill to die. He was saved by a she-bear who fed him her milk until he was found by a herdsman who cared for him.

The judgement of Paris

This story starts at the wedding of **Thetis** and **Peleus** (page 23). It tells how **Eris**, the goddess of spite, took her revenge for not being invited.

Eris arrived during the feast with an apple inscribed, "For the fairest." **Hera, Athene** and **Aphrodite** all reached for it. **Zeus** did not want to choose between them, imagining the fury of the two not chosen. He decided someone else must judge and picked Paris.

Paris was guarding his foster-father's sheep when **Hermes** arrived with the goddesses and asked Paris to choose the loveliest.

Each goddess tried to bribe Paris: Hera with power and wealth; Athene with great victories and wisdom; but Aphrodite just smiled and promised him the love of the most beautiful woman in the world if he chose her. Paris could not resist Aphrodite and gave her the apple, earning the hatred of Hera and Athene.

Aphrodite said that the most beautiful woman in the world was Helen and that she lived in Greece at the court of **Menelaus** of Sparta. She did not say that Helen was Menelaus's wife.

Paris returns to Troy

Soon after, Paris competed in some Games in Troy and won more prizes than any Trojan prince. Afraid that someone might harm Paris out of jealousy, his foster-father revealed who he really was. The Trojans welcomed him, forgetting the prophesy.

Helen

Helen's parents were Zeus and **Leda** (see page 23). All the Greek princes wanted to marry

her. Her foster-father, **Tyndareus**, cleverly made all the suitors swear to support the man picked as her husband, then chose Menelaus.

Earlier, the Greeks had kidnapped Princess **Hesione** of Troy, Priam's sister. Priam sent Paris with some men to arrange her release and agreed that if the Greeks did not comply, they would seize a Greek princess in return.

Helen had never loved Menelaus, and when Paris came to Sparta she fell in love with him, as Aphrodite had promised. She agreed to run off with him, so the Trojans returned with a Greek princess as planned.

Menelaus was furious when Helen disappeared. He knew she had left willingly and that his own men had started the trouble by kidnapping Hesione, but he could not accept the insult. He asked his brother, **Agamemnon**, and Helen's former suitors to help get her back.

The suitors

Many of the suitors did not want to go to war, despite their promise to support Helen's husband. One, **Odysseus**, pretended to be mad when Menelaus's men came to fetch him. He started ploughing the beach but they placed his baby son, **Telemachus**, in his path and Odysseus swerved, proving he was sane.

At last, a thousand ships were prepared and armed to go to war against Troy.

The Trojans were willing to go to war for Helen because she had charmed them all. Only **Cassandra**, Paris's sister, predicted disaster. She could see the future, but had displeased **Apollo**, who cursed her never to be believed.

Eris's revenge

The Greek fleet was held up for lack of wind and this was when Agamemnon sacrificed his daughter, **Iphigenia** (see page 17). The wind changed at last and they sailed to Troy. The Trojans would not return Helen so the war, which was Eris's spiteful revenge, began.

THE TROJAN WAR

The war dragged on for ten years. The Greeks could not break into Troy and the Trojans could not drive them off.

Aeneas

Many heroes were killed on both sides. One great Trojan hero was **Aeneas, Aphrodite's** son by **Anchises**. He was wounded by **Diomedes** and Aphrodite rushed to help him. Diomedes stopped her and even dared graze her with his spear. In the end, Apollo carried him to **Leto** and **Artemis**, who healed him.

Achilles

The most famous Greek warrior was **Achilles**. He was one of the seven sons of **Thetis** and **Peleus**. She made six of her sons immortal by burning away their mortal half. She was doing the same for the baby Achilles, when Peleus came in. He thought she was hurting the child and prevented her finishing, so Achilles was left with one vulnerable place on his body where he could be fatally wounded – the heel by which Thetis had held him.

Achilles was given the choice of a long, undistinguished life or a short but glorious one. He chose the second.

As time went on, the warriors began to quarrel. Achilles argued with **Agamemnon** over a slave girl and left the battle, sulking. The Greeks lost heart and were driven back by the Trojan hero **Hector, Priam's** son.

The deaths of three heroes

In desperation **Patroclus** put on Achilles's armour and led an attack. He was not as skilled as Achilles, though, the Trojans saw through his disguise and Hector killed him. Achilles was stricken with guilt and sorrow and plunged back into battle. He killed Hector and dragged his body round the city behind his chariot before letting the Trojans buy it back for burial.

Paris emerged to avenge Hector's death and shot Achilles in the heel – his only weak spot – and killed him.

Ajax kills himself

Ajax and **Odysseus** disputed who should inherit Achilles's armour, as they had both guarded his body during the battle. Agamemnon decided Odysseus should have it and Ajax killed himself in shame. To prevent more trouble, Odysseus gave the armour to Achilles's son **Neoptolemus**.

With many of their heroes dead, the Greeks were told that only the famous archer **Philoctetes** could save them.

Philoctetes brings new hope

Philoctetes had been on his way to Troy when he was bitten by a snake. His wound was not fatal, but would not heal, so the Greeks had left him behind. He felt very bitter about this treatment and when the Greeks came back to beg for his help he refused at first. Then **Heracles** came to him in a dream, saying that if he forgave the Greeks and went to Troy, his wound would heal. He returned with them and killed Paris with a skillful shot, which gave the Greeks new hope. At once the snake bite began to heal as Heracles had promised.

The Trojan horse

Troy finally fell thanks to a trick thought up by Odysseus. The Greeks pretended to give up. They built a huge wooden horse as a gift to **Athene**, so she would grant them a safe trip home. They left it outside the gates of Troy and sailed away. The Trojans were overjoyed. They pulled the horse through the city gates and offered it at their own temple of Athene.

That night they celebrated, but when they were all asleep, some Greeks who had hidden inside the hollow horse slipped out of the trapdoor in its side. They opened the city gates to let in the Greek army, who had sneaked back under cover of darkness.

The Greeks ransacked Troy and vast numbers of Trojans were killed. **Helen** was captured and taken to **Menelaus**. He intended to punish her but despite all the bloodshed she had caused, he found he still loved her and took her back as his wife.

AFTER THE TROJAN WAR

The trick of the wooden horse (page 43) ended the Trojan War. **Paris** had caused the destruction of Troy, as predicted, and the surviving Greeks went home. But for some of the characters their adventures did not end with the war.

Aeneas and the Palladium

Aeneas was one of the few Trojan nobles who survived. He escaped from Troy with a sacred statue called the Palladium. It was a gift from **Athene** and it was said that wherever it stood would be the centre of a great empire.

After many travels Aeneas settled in Italy. His descendants were supposed to have been present at the founding of Rome and to have placed the Palladium in a Roman temple. Rome did become the capital of an empire and Julius Caesar claimed descent from Aeneas and his mother, Venus (**Aphrodite's** Roman name).

Agamemnon's return

Agamemnon was a descendant of **Tantalus** (see page 27), and was thus subject to **Zeus's** curse on his family. The fates of Agamemnon and his son, **Orestes**, illustrate the Greeks' belief in retribution, by which you reaped the rewards or punishments of your own behaviour, or that of your ancestors.

After the war, Agamemnon went home to Mycenae where his wife, **Clytemnestra**, was waiting for him. She hated Agamemnon. He had killed her first husband and married her by force. He sacrificed their daughter, **Iphigenia**, for a favourable wind to go to war (Clytemnestra did not know about the rescue by **Artemis** – see page 17) and then stayed away fighting for ten years. Clytemnestra plotted her revenge with Agamemnon's cousin, **Aegisthus**, who had always wanted to be king himself.

Agamemnon brought **Cassandra** (see page 41) home with him as a slave. She had already given birth to his twin sons and when Clytemnestra saw them she was even more determined to punish her husband.

Pretending to welcome him home, Clytemnestra offered the weary Agamemnon a hot bath. He accepted, paying no attention to Cassandra's warnings of danger which, as usual, were not believed. When he had taken off his clothes and armour and was defenceless, Clytemnestra stabbed him to death. She killed Cassandra and her twins, too, and married Aegisthus. They ruled as king and queen and seemed to have got away with their crimes.

Orestes and the Oracle

Clytemnestra and Agamemnon had children other than Iphigenia. Their son, **Orestes**, was being brought up at his grandparents' home, so he did not witness the murder of his father. Their daughter, **Electra**, was not so lucky. She had to live with the murderess and her new husband and watch them do well.

When he grew older, Orestes received a command from the Delphic **Oracle** to avenge his father's death. He was horrified, but went home with his cousin, **Pylades**, to find out what was going on.

Electra soon convinced him that their mother was guilty and should be punished. Spurred on by her hatred, Orestes killed Clytemnestra and Aegisthus. Thus their evil deeds were punished.

Retribution

However, killing your mother, no matter what she had done, was the worst possible crime. The avenging **Furies** (see page 8) soon came hunting Orestes and drove him mad with grief and remorse. It was no excuse that **Apollo** himself had ordered the murder through his Oracle.

Orestes was driven to wandering through Greece. In Sparta he tried to kill **Helen** as she had caused so much misery but Zeus came down, wrapped her in a cloud and took her to Olympus to be a goddess.

In Athens Orestes begged to be put on trial. Athene was the judge and Apollo himself appeared to defend Orestes. Athene decided Orestes had suffered enough and ordered the Furies to leave him alone. Three of them did so but the rest continued to pursue him.

The Oracle next told Orestes to sail to the land of the Taurians and bring back a statue of Artemis they had. The Taurians were barbarians who sacrificed strangers but Orestes and Pylades set off anyway. They were captured and prepared for sacrifice but when the priestess came to kill them, it was Iphigenia. She had been brought there by Artemis when she was saved from death. She recognized her brother and helped him and Pylades escape with the statue.

The curse is lifted

At last Orestes had made amends for his crime, the curse on his family was lifted and he was left in peace. Iphigenia continued as a priestess of Artemis, Pylades married Electra and Orestes married **Hermione**, daughter of Helen and **Menelaus**.

THE ADVENTURES OF ODYSSEUS

Odysseus lived on the island of Ithaca with his wife, **Penelope**, and son, **Telemachus**. He had been warned that if he went to Troy he would not return for twenty years. He tried to avoid going (see page 41) but it was no use, as he had sworn to help **Menelaus**.

The Odyssey

Odysseus fought at Troy for ten years, and it was his idea for the wooden horse that ended the war. His journey home was full of mishaps, which were recounted in **Homer's** poem, The Odyssey.

First, his ship was separated from the rest in a storm. It was washed up in the land of the **Lotus-eaters** (Libya). Eating lotus-fruit made you forget everything except the desire to eat more fruit. Some sailors succumbed and had to be dragged back to the ship.

They called at the island of the **Cyclops, Polyphemus**, who shut them in a cave with his sheep and began to eat them one by one.

The sheep went out to graze each morning but the giant never let a man slip out, too. Eventually, Odysseus found a stick and used it to blind Polyphemus while he slept. When the sheep went out next morning, the men clung to their bellies. The blind Cyclops felt each sheep to make sure no-one escaped on their backs, but did not think to feel underneath them. When he discovered the trick, Polyphemus asked **Poseidon** to avenge him.

Not long after, the crew were entertained by **Aeolus**, guardian of the winds (see page 48). He tied the storm winds in a bag and gave them to Odysseus to keep. His foolish men thought the bag contained treasure and opened it, releasing a tempest.

They were driven onto Aeaea, home of **Circe**, a witch. She turned unwanted visitors into pigs and this was the fate of the first men sent for help by Odysseus. **Hermes** gave Odysseus a flower that made him immune to Circe's spells. He demanded the release of his men. Circe was impressed by his boldness and fell in love with him. She restored his men and they stayed with her for a while. She had three sons with Odysseus, though he remained keen to go home.

Circe sent him to the Underworld to consult **Tiresias** (see page 15) about his future. The seer warned him that when he got home he would find men fighting over his goods.

They finally left Aeaea, sailing safely past the **sirens** (see page 33) by blocking their ears with wax, except for Odysseus who wanted to hear their voices. He had himself tied to the mast so he could not be lured to them.

Still the dangers were not over. They had to negotiate a narrow channel between two monsters it was almost impossible to avoid. One was the **Scylla**, who had six heads and snapping dogs at her waist. The other was the whirlpool **Charybdis** which sucked ships to their doom. Odysseus chose to pass nearer the Scylla and just got by, though she killed some of his men.

On Sicily the sailors killed and ate some of the cattle of the **Titan, Hyperion**. Tiresias had warned Odysseus not to harm these sacred animals and the angry gods sank his ship, drowning all the men. Odysseus survived by clinging to the mast.

He was washed up on the island of Ortygia, where **Thetis's** daughter, **Calypso**, ruled. She stopped Odysseus leaving for seven years until Zeus sent Hermes to make her let him go.

At last he reached the shores of Ithaca and entered his court disguised as an old man.

He found things as Tiresias had predicted. The nobles were squandering his wealth and trying to make Penelope re-marry. She knew that if Odysseus was dead it would be wise to accept one of them but she delayed choosing, claiming she must finish her weaving first. She wove all day, then undid her work at night. This ruse was eventually discovered and she was forced to complete the cloth.

Odysseus revealed his true identity to his son, Telemachus, and they secretly removed all the nobles' weapons from the hall.

Penelope said she would marry the man who could string the bow Odysseus had left behind and shoot an arrow. She was sure no-one could do it. The suitors tried but failed. Odysseus then came forward. They laughed at the "old man" but he easily strung the bow and shot an arrow. Realizing who he must be, they reached for their weapons, only to find they were gone. Odysseus had no pity and killed them all.

Odysseus settled down again with his family, but one day a strange ship arrived. Odysseus attacked, thinking they were raiders. He was killed in the fight and only afterwards was it discovered that the strangers were led by his own son, one of Circe's children.

MORE HEROES

There are many more heroes and stories which there has not been room to include – some of them are briefly mentioned here.

Aeolus, keeper of the winds

Aeolus was keeper of the winds. He was supposed to let them loose one at a time but they were often hard to control. The **East Wind, Eurus**, was violent and disorderly; **Boreas**, the **North Wind** (see page 30), was cold and blustery; **Auster** was the hot, rainy **South Wind** and the gentle **West Wind** was called **Zephyr**.

Handsome humans

The gods sometimes picked out especially attractive humans as friends. Here are the stories of two of them:

Ganymede, the son of King **Tros** of Troy, was a very handsome youth. **Zeus** sent an eagle to pluck him from Earth to become an Immortal on Olympus. He took over as cup-bearer to the gods from the goddess, **Hebe**, and his image was placed among the stars as **Aquarius**, the water-carrier.

Hyacinthus was a Spartan prince. He was also strikingly good-looking and became **Apollo's** companion. The West Wind was jealous of their friendship and when Apollo was teaching Hyacinthus to throw the discus, the wind caught up the heavy disc and flung it back at the prince, killing him. Where his blood fell the first hyacinth flowers grew.

Creon

Creon drove **Oedipus** from Thebes, took the crown and became king in his place. Oedipus's sons rebelled, but were killed. Creon forbade them proper burial, which meant their spirits could not find peace. Their sister, **Antigone**, secretly sought their bodies and performed the burial ceremony. Creon condemned her to death, but his own son, **Haemon**, saved and married her.

Hellen

Hellen was the son of **Deucalion** and grandson of **Prometheus**. The Greeks claimed him as their ancestor, calling themselves Hellenes. There were four Hellenic races: Aeolians, from **Aeolus**, Hellen's eldest son; Dorians, from **Dorus**, his youngest; Ionians and Achaeans from his grandsons, **Ion** and **Achaeus**.

Aristaeus

He was the bee-keeping son of Apollo and the water-nymph, **Cyrene**. He made advances to **Orpheus's** wife, **Eurydice**, and she was running away from him when she received her fatal snake bite (see page 31). As punishment for causing her death, his bees died and he had to make sacrifices to Orpheus and Eurydice to make amends.

Aristaeus was the father of **Actaeon**, who was torn to pieces by **Artemis's** hounds (see page 17). After his son's death he travelled to Sardinia, Sicily and Thrace, where he was worshipped as a god.

Arion

Legend says that **Arion's** father was **Poseidon** and his mother a **nymph**, though he may have been based on a real poet. He was a skilled musician and in one contest he won so many prizes that, on his way home, some sailors threw him overboard, meaning to steal his treasure. Luckily, his playing had attracted several dolphins and one of them took Arion on his back and swam him safely home.

Daedalus

Daedalus was a craftsman at King **Minos's** court. He was a noble Athenian but had fled Greece after murdering someone. He later offended Minos and was imprisoned. His escape is described on page 26.

Hoping to recapture Daedalus, Minos issued a challenge: that no-one could pass a linen thread through a Triton shell. It was almost impossible, as the shells have spiral insides. Minos knew that if anyone could do it, Daedalus could and he was right. Daedalus tied the thread to an ant, which he sent through the shell, drawing the thread behind it. He was not recaptured, though.

Calchas

Calchas was a Trojan who joined the Greeks against his own countrymen. He was a great seer and predicted many of the events in the Trojan Wars. He is supposed to have died of humiliation when he met **Mopsus**, a seer wiser than himself.

Pelops

Pelops was the unfortunate son that **Tantalus** served to the gods for dinner (see page 27). The gods punished Tantalus and brought Pelops back to life, giving him an ivory shoulder to replace the one **Demeter** had absent-mindedly chewed.

Pelops wanted to marry **Hippodamia**, daughter of King **Oenomaus**. The king had been told he would be killed by his son-in-law so he challenged suitors to a chariot race in which the loser was executed. No-one had yet beaten him, but Poseidon lent Pelops some winged horses, while Pelops bribed the charioteer **Myrtilus** to sabotage the king's chariot.

Oenomaus was killed in a huge crash. Pelops, his bride and Myrtilus escaped, but Pelops ungratefully threw Myrtilus into the sea. This renewed the curse which Tantalus had earned for his family, and it was passed on to his grandson, **Agamemnon**. It was only lifted by his great-grandson, **Orestes** (see pages 44-45).

Cadmus

Cadmus was **Europa's** brother (see page 22). He went looking for her after Zeus stole her away and had many adventures. Once, he killed a serpent of Apollo's, as it had slain his men. **Athene** told him to plant the serpent's teeth and when he did, armed warriors sprang up. Cadmus set them fighting each other and when there were only five left alive he took them into his service to replace his men.

WHO'S WHO IN THE GREEK MYTHS

This section is a Who's Who of characters and monsters in the Greek myths. Any character whose name appears in bold type in this book has an entry here and there are some extra entries that do not appear in these stories but which you may come across elsewhere. The

Who's Who tells you about the family, doings, personality, appearance and magic powers of each character. It is arranged alphabetically and some abbreviations have been used to save space. You can find out how to understand the entries in the example below.

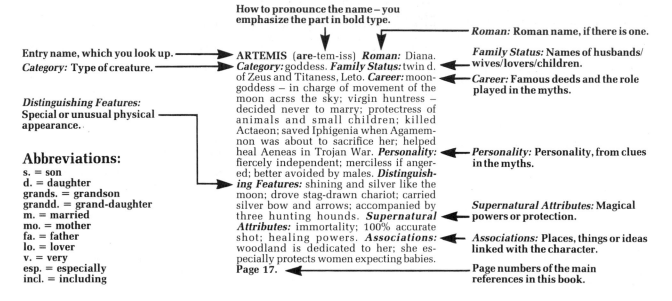

How to pronounce the name – you emphasize the part in bold type.

Roman: Roman name, if there is one.

Entry name, which you look up.
Category: Type of creature.

ARTEMIS (are-tem-iss) *Roman:* Diana. *Category:* goddess. *Family Status:* twin d. of Zeus and Titaness, Leto. *Career:* moon-goddess – in charge of movement of the moon acrss the sky; virgin huntress – decided never to marry; protectress of animals and small children; killed Actaeon; saved Iphigenia when Agamemnon was about to sacrifice her; helped heal Aeneas in Trojan War. *Personality:* fiercely independent; merciless if angered; better avoided by males. *Distinguishing Features:* shining and silver like the moon; drove stag-drawn chariot; carried silver bow and arrows; accompanied by three hunting hounds. *Supernatural Attributes:* immortality; 100% accurate shot; healing powers. *Associations:* woodland is dedicated to her; she especially protects women expecting babies. **Page 17.**

Family Status: Names of husbands/wives/lovers/children.

Career: Famous deeds and the role played in the myths.

Distinguishing Features: Special or unusual physical appearance.

Personality: Personality, from clues in the myths.

Abbreviations:
s. = son
d. = daughter
grands. = grandson
grandd. = grand-daughter
m. = married
mo. = mother
fa. = father
lo. = lover
v. = very
esp. = especially
incl. = including

Supernatural Attributes: Magical powers or protection.

Associations: Places, things or ideas linked with the character.

Page numbers of the main references in this book.

ACAMAS (ak-a-mass) *Category:* mortal. *Family Status:* s. of Theseus and Phaedra; lo. of Phyllis (relationship tragically ended before marriage due to her broken heart). *Career:* military hero; was one of the soldiers who hid in the Trojan horse. *Personality:* career-minded, to the detriment of his personal life; faithful. **Page 30.**

ACHAEUS (a-kee-us) see **HELLEN.**

ACHILLES (a-kill-eez) *Category:* mortal. *Family Status:* s. of Peleus and Thetis; lo. of Deidameia; one s. Neoptolemus. *Career:* hero; chose glorious life and early death; important (if erratic) military commander for Greeks in Trojan War; abandoned battle at crucial point, but returned for vengeance when his friend, Patroclus, was killed; slew Hector; received fatal wound in heel from Paris. *Personality:* v. brave and eager to excell in battle; jealous of his position; staunch friend when roused; fond of women; prone to moodiness and sulking. *Distinguishing Features:* swift of foot. *Supernatural Attributes:* invulnerable to all weapons, except for one spot on his heel. *Associations:* someone's physical or emotional weak spot can be called his "Achilles' heel"; the tendon in your heel that joins your foot to your calf is called the "Achilles' tendon". **Page 42.**

ACRISIUS (a-kriss-ee-us) *Category:* mortal. *Family Status:* nephew of

Hyacinthus; one d. Danae; one grands. Perseus. *Career:* king; blighted by prophecy that he would be killed by his grands.; set Danae and baby Perseus adrift on the sea but could not avoid Fate; was killed accidentally by Perseus. during a discus-throwing contest. **Page 22.**

ACTAEON (act-ee-on) *Category:* mortal. *Family Status:* s. of Aristaeus. *Career:* successful huntsman; made rare sighting of Artemis bathing; she turned him into a stag and he was hunted and killed by his own hounds. *Personality:* inquisitive; rash. *Distinguishing Features:* excellent bowman. **Page 17.**

ADONIS (a-don-iss) *Category:* mortal. *Family Status:* lo. of Aphrodite; lo. of Persephone. *Career:* affairs with goddesses attracted unwelcome attention from jealous Ares; killed by Ares in disguise as a boar; thanks to Aphrodite's pleading, he spent summers on Earth with her. *Personality:* carefree; popular with women. *Associations:* anemone flowers sprang up where his blood fell. **Page 13.**

AEETES (aye-ee-teez) *Category:* mortal. *Family Status:* one s.; one d. Medea. *Career:* King of Colchis; obstructed Jason's quest for golden fleece; made attempt on Jason's life by asking him to harness fire-breathing bulls and plant dragon's teeth; gave chase when Jason left

with fleece; persecution of Jason ended by brutal murder of his s. by Medea. *Personality:* sly; cunning. **Page 32.**

AEGEUS (ij-ee-us) *Category:* mortal. *Family Status:* one s. Theseus (by magic); m. Medea; one s. *Career:* King of Athens; drove Medea away after she tried to poison Theseus; early misfortune in being responsible for death of King Minos's son led to terrible debt – 7 young men and 7 girls sent to Crete every 9 years to be sacrificed to the Minotaur; drowned himself soon after seeing Theseus's ship return from Crete with black sails raised, the sign that Theseus was dead. *Personality:* anxious; depressive. *Associations:* place where he drowned named Aegean Sea after him. **Page 34**

AEGISTHUS (ee-giss-thus) *Category:* mortal. *Family Status:* cousin of Agamemnon; m. Clytemnestra (unlawfully, as she had been m. to Agamemnon and it was not permitted to marry such a close relative's former husband or wife). *Career:* quarrelled with Agamemnon over throne of Mycenae; became king by criminal means – accomplice in murder of Agamemnon; executed by his step-s., Orestes. *Personality:* heartless, bitter and ambitious. **Page 44.**

AEGYPTUS (ee-jip-tus) *Category:* mortal. *Family Status:* grands. of Poseidon; 50 s. *Career:* famous for attempted mass-murder of his brother, Danaus, and Danaus's 50 daughters; plot foiled by proposed victims. **Personality:** greedy, cruel. **Associations:** Egypt named after him. **Page 25.**

AENEAS (in-**ee**-us) **Category:** mortal. **Family Status:** s. of Anchises and Aphrodite; lo. of Dido. **Career:** great hero; warrior for Troy in Trojan War; wounded by Diomedes, healed by Leto and Artemis; escaped fall of Troy with his fa. and small son; fled to Italy with Palladium; descendants founded Rome; doomed love affair with Dido, whom he abandoned. **Personality:** tremendous courage tempered by survival instinct. **Supernatural Attributes:** enjoys special protection of his mo., Aphrodite. **Pages 42, 44,**

AEOLUS (ee-**ole**-us) **Category:** god **Family Status:** fa. of Alcyone. **Career:** keeper of the winds; gave captured storm winds to Odysseus in a bag so he would only have fair winds. **Personality:** generally helpful, but not always able to control his charges. **Supernatural Attributes:** immortality. **Associations:** Aeolian Islands (NW of Sicily) named after him; Aeolian harp – instrument with strings which make music when wind blows across them. **Pages 46, 48.**

AGAMEMNON (ag-a-**mem**non) **Category:** mortal. **Family Status:** descendant of Atreus; m. Clytemnestra by force; one s. Orestes; three d. Electra, Iphigenia, Chrysothemis; brother of Menelaus. **Career:** King of Mycenae; soldier; commander of Greek troops in Trojan War; sacrificed Iphigenia; quarrelled with Achilles; took Cassandra slave; assassinated by Clytemnestra. **Personality:** violent and aggressive; argumentative; ruthless, even to his family; tactless. **Associations:** Heinrich Schliemann (on p. 40) thought he had found gold mask of Agamemnon amongst treasures at Mycenae – it actually turned out to be much older. **Page 44.**

AGAVE (a-**garv**-ee) **Category:** mortal. **Family Status:** mo. of Pentheus. **Career:** Queen of Thebes; Maenad (worshipper of Dionysus); killed Pentheus while under influence of religious trance. **Personality:** religious fanatic; best avoided, espcially by men, during religious ceremonies. **Supernatural Attributes:** superhuman strength in religious-induced frenzy; aid from Dionysus. **Page 19.**

AJAX (**age**-axe) **Category:** mortal. **Career:** mighty hero for Greeks in Trojan War; quarrelled with Odysseus over Achilles's armour; wasteful death by suicide. **Personality:** very strong but not too bright; obsessed with honour. **Page 42.**

ALCMENE (alk-**meen**-ee) **Category:** mortal. **Family Status:** m. Amphitryon; unwilling lo. of Zeus; one s. Heracles (fa. Zeus). **Career:** faithful wife, until tricked by Zeus. **Personality:** loyal. **Page 23.**

AMAZONS (**am**-a-zonz) **Category:** mortals. **Family Status:** descended from Ares and a naiad; do not generally marry, but have children by arrangement, involving no ties to the father. **Career:** fierce warriors; supported Troy in Trojan War; prevented Heracles taking their queen's girdle and he had to fight all of them. **Personalities:** ferocious; excellent shots. **Distinguishing Features:** female race; sometimes said to cut right breast off for ease of pulling bowstring; lived near the Black Sea. **Page 36.**

AMPHITRITE (am-fee-**try**-tee) **Category:** demi-goddess; nereid. **Family Status:** m. Poseidon; three children. **Career:** support to Poseidon; turned Scylla into a monster. **Distinguishing Features:** encountered by the sea. **Personality:** jealous. **Page 11.**

ANCHISES (an-**kye**-seez) **Category:** mortal. **Family Status:** lo. of Aphrodite; one s. Aeneas. **Career:** King of Dardanians; revealed his affair with Aphrodite so punished by Zeus. **Personality:** unable to keep a secret. **Distinguishing Features:** v. handsome. **Page 13.**

ANDROMEDA (an-**drom**-med-a) **Category:** mortal. **Family Status:** d. of King of Ethiopia; m. Perseus. **Career:** princess; her foolish parents boasted she was lovelier than the nereids; to appease Poseidon she was chained to a rock as sacrifice to a sea-monster; dramatic rescue in nick of time by Perseus. **Personality:** obedient, innocent. **Distinguishing Features:** beautiful as the nereids (almost). **Page 24.**

ANTIGONE (an-**tig**-on-ee) **Category:** mortal. **Family Status:** d. of Oedipus and Jocasta; lo. of Haemon. **Career:** acted as guide to Oedipus after he blinded himself; searched for and buried her brothers' bodies when killed in battle; condemned to death by Creon; hanged herself; Haemon stabbed himself when he found her dead. **Personality:** noble, brave and self-sacrificing; great loyalty to family and duty. **Pages 29, 48.**

APHRODITE (aff-ro-die-tee) **Roman:** Venus. **Category:** goddess. **Family Status:** d. of Uranus – born from foam caused by his blood dropping in the Ocean; m. Hephaestos; lo. of Ares; lo. of Anchises; lo. of Adonis and others; two s. Eros (fa. Ares?), Aeneas (fa. Anchises); one d. Harmonia (fa. Ares). **Career:** goddess of love; no formal duties except being lovely; competitive with Hera and Athene; responsible for Trojan War, as she promised Helen to Paris if he judged her fairest of the goddesses; fought for Troy in Trojan War, although it was unusual for her to take part in warfare; was wounded by Diomedes; brought about death of Adonis by arguing with Persephone over him and rousing Ares's jealousy; caused death of Glaucus by driving his horses mad; brought the statue, Galatea, to life for Pygmalion for his loyalty to true love. **Personality:** irresistibly charming; large appetite for lovers but fickle in affections; vain and competitive about her beauty. **Distinguishing Features:** exceeding beauty; usually accompanied by doves and sparrows, her special birds. **Supernatural Attributes:** immortality; girdle which makes everyone fall in love with the wearer – can be lent to humans. **Associations:** she was closely associated with Cyprus where she arrived soon after she was born. **Pages 12, 13.**

APOLLO (a-**poll**-o) **Category:** god. **Family Status:** twin s. of Zeus and Titaness, Leto; lo. of Calliope, the Muse; lo. of Coronis; lo. of Cyrene and others; three s. Orpheus (mo. Calliope), Asclepius (mo. Coronis), Aristaeus (mo. Cyrene). **Career:** sun god – in charge of the sun's movement across the sky; hunter; god and patron of the Arts – skilled musician on the lyre; tamed the Muses; killed the Python; famous for Oracles, prophecies told through his priests and priestesses; killed Marsyas after music contest; chased Daphne unsuccessfully. **Personality:** proud; protective towards his mother and sister; artistic; could be cruel. **Distinguishing Features:** carries gold bow and arrows; appears gold and shining, like the sun; wears laurel wreath in memory of Daphne. **Supernatural Attributes:** immortality; healing powers. **Associations:** small groups of trees were sacred to him; the raven was his bird. **Page 16.**

AQUARIUS (a-**kware**-ee-us) see **GANYMEDE.**

ARACHNE (a-**rack**-nee) **Category:** mortal. **Career:** skilled weaver; cut short in her prime by foolish boasting that she wove better than Athene; driven to suicide to avoide Athene's wrath; was turned into a spider so that her spinning skill would not be lost. **Personality:** highly-skilled but thoughtless. **Distinguishing Features:** expert web-weaving after transformation. **Page 15.**

ARES (**are**-eez) **Roman:** Mars. **Category:** god. **Family Status:** s. of Zeus and Hera; twin sister, Eris; lo. of Aphrodite; one s. Eros (mo. Aphrodite); one d. Harmonia (mo. Aphrodite). **Career:** god of war; involvement in all war-like activities, regardless of merit; will intervene on opposing sides if possible; took the shape of a boar and killed Adonis. **Personality:** violent and eager for a fight; revels in bloodshed; undependable ally as indifferent to the rights and wrongs of a dispute; expert but jealous lover (according to Aphrodite). **Distinguishing Features:** young, strong and handsome; preference for battle-gear. **Supernatural Attributes:** immortality; shape-changing. **Associations:** the Areopagus (Hill of Ares), situated NW of the Acropolis (Athens), was location for important trials. **Page 12.**

ARGONAUTS (**are**-go-norts) **Category:** mortals. **Family Status:** varied, but mostly noble. **Career:** many of them did other famous deeds but all were members of crew of Jason's ship, Argo; sailed with Jason on quest for golden fleece; drove off the Harpies; negotiated Clashing Rocks; resisted singing of Sirens; helped kill Talos. **Personalities:** tough; hungry for glory. **Distinguishing Features:** heavily armed. **Page 32.**

ARGUS (**are**-gus) **Category:** monster. **Family Status:** Hera's servant. **Career:** doing Hera's bidding; set to guard Io; killed Echidne; lulled to sleep and killed by Hermes. **Distinguishing Features:** 100 eyes, never all closed at once. **Associations:** after his death, Hera set his eyes in tail of the peacock, which became her symbol. **Page 22.**

ARIADNE (a-ree-**add**-nee) *Category:* mortal. *Family Status:* d. of Minos and Pasiphae; lo. of Theseus; m. Dionysus; six s. *Career:* Cretan princess; helped Theseus kill Minotaur; left Crete with him; abandoned by him on Naxos; rescued by and m. Dionysus; called down punishment on Theseus for abandoning her – caused death of his father, Aegeus. *Personality:* daring; vengeful; passionate. **Page 36.**

ARION (a-**rye**-on) *Category:* mortal. *Career:* musician; made good living by playing lyre; won many contests; was mugged for his winnings by some sailors; saved by dolphins. *Personality:* easygoing, lucky. **Page 49.**

ARISTAEUS (a-riss-**tay**-us) *Category:* demi-god. *Family Status:* s. of Apollo and water-nymph, Cyrene; three s. incl. Actaeon; one d. *Career:* bee-keeper; chased Eurydice to her death in the woods; as punishment, the gods made his bees die until he made sacrifices to atone; travelled widely after death of Actaeon and worshipped as a god. *Personality:* persistent; insensitive. *Supernatural Attributes:* immortality.

ARTEMIS (**are**-tem-iss) *Roman:* Diana. *Category:* goddess. *Family Status:* twin d. of Zeus and Titaness, Leto. *Career:* moon-goddess – in charge of movement of the moon acrss the sky; virgin huntress – decided never to marry; protectress of animals and small children; killed Actaeon; saved Iphigenia when Agamemnon was about to sacrifice her; helped heal Aeneas in Trojan War. *Personality:* fiercely independent; merciless if angered; better avoided by males. *Distinguishing Features:* shining and silver like the moon; drove stag-drawn chariot; carried silver bow and arrows; accompanied by three hunting hounds. *Supernatural Attributes:* immortality; 100% accurate shot; healing powers. *Associations:* woodland is dedicated to her; she especially protects women expecting babies. **Page 17.**

ASCLEPIUS (ass-**kleep**-ee-us) *Category:* god. *Family Status:* s. of Apollo and Coronis; two s; four d. incl. Panacea, Hygieia. . *Career:* god of medicine; v. successful doctor; went too far by bringing the dead back to life; killed by Zeus, then revived by him to become an Immortal. *Personality:* compassionate; proud of his powers, leading to showing-off; not respectful enough of the gods. *Supernatural Attributes:* immortality; healing powers, learnt from Apollo. *Associations:* his symbol – snakes twisted round a staff – became the symbol of pharmacy in many countries. **Page 16.**

ATHAMAS (**ath**-a-mass) *Category:* mortal. *Family Status:* m. Nephele, the cloud-woman; two s. incl. Phrixus; one d. Helle; m. Ino. *Career:* king; happy reign with Nephele but made big mistake when he put Nephele aside for Ino; tricked by Ino into sacrificing Phrixus – lost both his children by this act. *Personality:* good-natured but gullible. **Page 25.**

ATHENE (a-**thee**-nee) *Roman:* Minerva. *Category:* goddess. *Family Status:* d. of Zeus; born from his head, after he swallowed Titaness Metis in form of a fly; virgin goddess, never married *Career:* goddess of wisdom and war; preferred reason to violence, except when pushed; better warrior even than Ares; arbitrator of disputes; overseer of home crafts; inventor of flute; created olive tree and gave it to Greeks; blinded Tiresias, but gave him second sight to compensate; turned Medusa into a monster; turned Arachne into a spider for boasting she could weave better than her. *Personality:* v. wise; slow to anger, but highly dangerous if roused; competitive with other gods and humans. *Distinguishing Features:* always wore armour – especially noted for her helmet; carried Zeus's shield, the aegis; often called grey-eyed or flashing-eyed. *Supernatural Attributes:* unbeatable in combat; immortality. *Associations:* the owl is her bird; Athens named after her; also called Athene Parthenos and Pallas Athene. **Pages 14, 15.**

ATLAS (**at**-lass). *Category:* Titan. *Family Status:* s. of Uranus and Mother Earth; m. Hesperis, several d., the Hesperides. *Career:* one of the rulers of the world, under Uranus, until revolt of Zeus and the New Gods; fought with Uranus against Zeus; defeated, and punished by being made to support the heavens on his shoulders; almost escaped when he persuaded Heracles to take the weight while he went to fetch golden apples from his daughters, but was tricked into taking it back; turned to stone when shown Gorgon's head by Perseus. *Personality:* not too bright. *Distinguishing Features:* physical giant; massive strength. *Associations:* Atlas Mountains in Africa said to be where he was turned to stone.

AUGEUS (awe-**jee**-us) *Category:* mortal. *Career:* reputation based solely on filthiness of his stables, which had to be cleaned as one of the Twelve Labours of Heracles. *Personality:* uncaring to animals; slack in hygiene. **Page 39.**

AUSTER (**oss**-ter). *Category:* god. *Family Status:* kept in a bag, in the care of Aeolus. *Career:* South Wind; blew when and where released by Aeolus. *Personality:* hot and rainy. *Distinguishing Features:* body of a man; sometimes given a serpent's tail. *Supernatural Attributes:* immortality; flying like the wind. *Associations:* gave his name to Australia. **Page 48.**

BACCHAE (**back**-ee) See **MAENADS.**

BACCHUS (**back**-us) See **DIONYSUS.**

BELLEROPHON (bell-**air**-oh-fon) *Category:* mortal. *Family Status:* s. of Glaucus; grands. of Sisyphus. *Career:* served King Proteus of Argos; lost good reputation in scandal, although innocent; sent with letter demanding his own death to King of Lycia; made good impression and was not killed but asked to slay the Chimaera; gods lent him winged horse, Pegasus, and he succeeded; served King of Lycia faithfully; ruined promising career by attempting to fly to Olympus on Pegasus; struck down by Zeus. *Personality:* dashing and brave; responds well to adversity; cocksure and inclined to be over-confident. *Supernatural Attributes:* flying ability when he had the use of Pegasus. **Page 28.**

BOREAS (**bore**-ee-ass) *Category:* god. *Family Status:* in the care of Aeolus; m. Oreithyia *Career:* North Wind; blew as the gods directed; after marriage, special concern for city of Athens – scattered attacking Persian fleet. *Personality:* cold and blustery. *Distinguishing Features:* man's upper body, serpent's tail; sometimes winged and with two faces, looking forward and back. *Supernatural Attributes:* immortality. **Page 30.**

Boreas

BRONZE RACE *Category:* mortals. *Family Status:* created by Prometheus; forefathers of all humans. *Career:* their descendants were the heroes of Greek myths. *Personalities:* generally noble and good. *Distinguishing Features:* made in the image of the gods; first human-shaped life forms on Earth. **Page 20.**

CADMUS (**cad**-muss) *Category:* mortal. *Family Status:* brother of Europe; m. Harmonia; many children incl. d. Semele and Agave. *Career:* Phoenician prince and hero; life of enforced adventure while searching for Europa after she was carried off by Zeus; advised by Athene to plant serpent's teeth, from which sprang warriors which he took into his service; told by Oracle to follow a cow and found a city where it lay down; founded Thebes and ruled as king; went to Isles of the Blessed when he died. *Personality:* brave and dependable; good leader; inspired confidence. **Page 49.**

CALCHAS (**kal**-kass) *Category:* mortal. *Career:* seer and priest of Apollo; was Trojan but supported Greece in Trojan War; told future for Agamemnon; unusual death of mortification upon meeting Mopsus, a seer greater than himself. *Personality:* conscientious; proud of his powers; useful back-up to military commander; willing to be unpopular, as his predictions were often bad news. *Supernatural Attributes:* power to predict future events, given by Apollo. **Page 49.**

CALLISTO (cal-**iss**-toe) *Category:* demi-goddess; nymph *Family Status:* lo. of Zeus; one s. Arcas. *Career:* follower of Artemis; broke rules of chastity by falling in love with Zeus; turned into a bear by Artemis; hunted and killed; turned into star group, the Great Bear, by Zeus; Arcas was ancestor of Arcadians. *Personality:* simple, straightforward and rather unlucky. **Page 17.**

CALYPSO (cal-**ips**-oh) *Category:* demi-goddess; nymph. *Family Status:* d. of Atlas; lo. of Odysseus; possibly two/three s. (fa. Odysseus). *Career:* lived on island of Ortygia; fell in love with Odysseus when he called there on his travels; kept him with her by force for seven years; made to release him by Hermes on orders from Zeus. *Personality:* dominating; gets what she wants. *Supernatural Attributes:* long life; power to make mortals do what she wants. **Page 47.**

CASSANDRA (cass-**and**-ra) *Category:* mortal. *Family Status:* d. of King Priam and Queen Hecuba of Troy; slave and lo. of Agamemnon; twin s. (fa. Agamemnon). *Career:* Trojan princess; priestess of Apollo; seer; offended Apollo who cursed her never to be believed; tried to warn that Trojan War would bring disaster to Troy; taken prisoner by Agamemnon and returned to Mycenae with him; tried to warn him of Clytemnestra's murderous plans, but to no avail; slain by Clytemnestra. *Personality:* desperate and unhappy due to betraying Apollo; given to wailing and gnashing of teeth in despair. *Supernatural Attributes:* seeing future. *Associations:* someone (esp. female) who is always predicting bad news can be called a "Cassandra". **Page 41.**

CASTOR (**cass**-tor) *Category:* mortal. *Family Status:* twin s. of Tyndareus and Leda (his twin, Polydeuces, had Zeus as father, but the same mother and was born at the same time). *Career:* Argonaut; promising military skills, but killed young, along with his twin, in battle; went to Underworld as he was human, but Polydeuces went to Olympus as he was half-immortal; they could not bear separation and Polydeuces begged to go and join Castor in the Underworld; Zeus was touched and allowed them to spend alternate days in each place so they could be together. *Personality:* honourable, courageous; strong on family loyalty. *Distinguishing Features:* nearly always with his twin. *Associations:* sometimes called the Dioscuri; their image is set in the stars as Gemini, the twins.

CENTAURS (**sen**-tors) *Category:* demigods. *Family Status:* grands. of Ixion and Nephele. *Career:* usually employed as teachers of heroes; caused riot at a Lapith wedding. *Personalities:* wise, patient, brave but unreliable if given too much wine. *Distinguishing Features:* male human head and top half of body, bottom half of body and legs of a horse. *Supernatural Attributes:* unrivalled ability to teach riding, shooting bow and arrows and give advice at same time.

Centaur

Cerberus

CERBERUS (**sir**-ber-us) *Category:* monster. *Family Status:* child of Typhon and Echidne; Pluto's servant. *Career:* guarding gates of Underworld to prevent the dead leaving; was dragged to Earth to court of King Eurystheus as one of Twelve Labours of Heracles. *Personality:* ferocious; fond of snapping jaws and slaver-

ing; much to be feared on a trip to the Underworld. *Distinguishing Features:* he is a dog with three heads. *Supernatural Attributes:* immortality; his spittle produces aconite flowers, which contain the poison, wolf's bane. **Page 39.**

CERES (**seer**-eez) see **DEMETER.**

CERYNEAN HIND (**sair**-ee-nee-an) *Category:* animal; deer. *Family Status:* sacred to Artemis. *Career:* caught by Heracles as one of his Twelve Labours. *Personality:* shy; elusive. *Distinguishing Features:* golden horns. *Supernatural Attributes:* super-fast, almost impossible to catch. **Page 38.**

CHARON (**ka**-ron) *Category:* servant to the gods. *Career:* ferryman who rowed the dead across the River Styx into the Underworld; his fee was one obol (Ancient Greek coin). *Personality:* fierce, bad-tempered and menacing; miserly. *Distinguishing Features:* a white-haired old man with blazing eyes; often wore a hooded cloak. *Supernatural Attributes:* immortality; unavoidable on the journey to the Underworld. *Associations:* the Greeks always buried their dead with an obol in their mouth to pay Charon.

CHARYBDIS (kar-**rib**-diss) *Category:* natural phenomenon. *Family Status:* child of Typhon and Echidne. *Career:* wrecking ships and drowning humans; encountered by Odysseus, who managed to escape. *Personality:* pitiless; does not discriminate between good and evil. *Distinguishing Features:* it is a gigantic whirlpool; the monster, Scylla, is normally close by. **Page 47.**

CHIMAERA (kim-**ear**-a) *Category:* monster. *Career:* killing and devouring humans. *Personality:* extremely fierce; lethal to all ordinary mortals, killed by hero, Bellerophon, and winged horse, Pegasus. *Distinguishing Features:* head of a lion, body of a goat, serpent's tail. *Supernatural Attributes:* fire-breathing. *Associations:* a wildly improbably thing can be described as a "chimaera". **Page 28.**

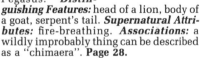

Chimaera

CIRCE (**sir**-see) *Category:* demi-goddess. *Family Status:* aunt of Medea; lo. of Odysseus; several s. (fa. Odysseus). *Career:* enchantress; practised magic on island of Aeaea; turned unwanted visitors into pigs; visited by Odysseus and used her spells on his men; impressed by Odysseus's courage and kept him as her lo. for a year; sent him to Underworld to consult Tiresias. *Personality:* lonely; wary; unreasonable to strangers. *Supernatural Attributes:* spell-casting. **Page 47.**

CLASHING ROCKS *Category:* natural phenomenon. *Career:* destroying sailors; positioned at entrance to Straits of Bosphorus; rocks clash shut if a ship tries to sail between them; attempted destruc-

tion of Jason and the Argonauts; also called Symplegades. *Personality:* impersonal will to destroy all mortals. *Distinguishing Features:* dark and menacing; craggy cliffs. *Supernatural Attributes:* opening and closing ability. **Page 32.**

CLYTEMNESTRA (kly-tem-**nest**-ra). *Category:* mortal. *Family Status:* d. of Tyndareus and Leda; m. Agamemnon against her will; one s. Orestes; three d. Iphigenia, Electra, Chrysothemis; m. Aegisthus. *Career:* Queen of Mycenae; became obsessed by hatred of Agamemnon; resulted in murder plot on his return from Trojan War; Aegisthus was her accomplice; killed in revenge by Orestes. *Personality:* embittered by experience; consumed with hatred of her husband. **Page 44.**

CREON (**kree**-on) *Category:* mortal. *Family Status:* brother of Jocasta; one s. Haemon; one d. Glauce. *Career:* King of Thebes after Oedipus; refused burial to Oedipus's son when he died in battle and threatened to punish Antigone when she found and buried him; killed in fire caused by Medea. *Personality:* strong and firm; somewhat unsympathetic. **Page 48.**

CRONOS (**kron**-oss) *Roman:* Saturn. *Category:* Titan. *Family Status:* s. of Uranus and Mother Earth; m. his sister, Titaness Rhea; three s. Poseidon, Pluto, Zeus; three d. Hera, Hestia, Demeter. *Career:* ruler of the world under Uranus; led rebellion against Uranus and became king of the gods; told he would be deposed by his own child so swallowed them all except the last one, Zeus, who was hidden from him; Zeus made him spew out his brothers and sisters then led a successful revolt against Cronos. *Personality:* mother-dominated; ruthless. *Distinguishing Features:* giant. *Supernatural Attributes:* immortality; gigantic strength. *Associations:* he is sometimes linked with Old Father Time with his scythe. **Page 8.**

Cyclops

CYCLOPES (**sye**-klo-peas) *Category:* demi-gods. *Family Status:* s. of Uranus and Mother Earth. *Career:* the original three were rejected and imprisoned in Tartarus by Uranus; rescued by Zeus; fought for Zeus against Titans; gave Zeus his thunderbolts, Pluto his helmet of invisibility and Poseidon his trident; killed by Apollo in revenge for death of Asclepius; their descendants lived on Sicily, working as shepherds or herdsmen; one of them, Polyphemus, imprisoned Odysseus when he visited. *Personality:* morose; bad-tempered. *Distinguishing Features:* giant size; one eye only in centre of forehead. *Supernatural Attributes:* extremely long life; enormous strength. **Pages 8, 46.**

DAEDALUS (**deed**-a-luss) *Category:* mortal. *Family Status:* one s. Icarus. *Career:* Athenian craftsman and inventor at court of King Minos; helped Minos's wife, Pasiphae, have love affair with a bull, resulting in birth of Minotaur; built Labyrinth to hold Minotaur; offended Minos, was imprisoned, but escaped by making wings of wax and feathers; passed linen thread through Triton shell by tying it to an ant. *Personality:* cunning; very clever with his hands; slippery customer. **Pages 26, 48.**

DANAE (**dan**-ee) *Category:* mortal. *Family Status:* d. of King Acrisius; lo. of Zeus; one s. Perseus. *Career:* princess; imprisoned by her father to prevent her marrying, as he was warned that he would be killed by his grandson; visited by Zeus as a shower of gold; gave birth to Perseus; set adrift in a boat with her son; Zeus guided them to Seriphos where King Polydictes looked after them; resisted advances of Polydictes for years; about to be forced to marry him when Perseus returned from adventures and turned him to stone, so she was free from his attentions. *Personality:* strong-willed. **Page 22.**

DANAUS (**dan**-eh-us) *Category:* mortal. *Family Status:* grands. of Poseidon; 50 d. *Career:* famous for inciting the mass-murder of his brother, Aegyptus's, 50 sons by his own daughters when they were forced to marry each other following a quarrel over their inheritance; daughters suitably punished in Tartarus. *Personality:* proud; unforgiving; careless of the penalties for killing relatives. **Page 25.**

DAPHNE (**daff**-nee) *Career:* demi-goddess; mountain-nymph. *Family Status:* d. of a river-god; refused to be lo. of Apollo. *Career:* priestess of Mother Earth; defended her virtue by running away from Apollo; prayed to Mother Earth for help and was turned into a laurel tree; Apollo wore laurel wreath in her memory. *Personality:* pure; virtuous. *Distinguishing Features:* lived in mountains; fast runner. *Supernatural Attributes:* long life. **Page 16.**

DEIANEIRA (day-a-**neer**-a) *Category:* mortal. *Family Status:* second wife of Heracles. *Career:* almost carried off by the Centaur, Nessus, but saved by Heracles; caused the death of Heracles by being tricked into giving him a shirt which she believed contained a charm to keep him faithful to her; it was actually poisoned, caused agony and was impossible to remove so Heracles killed himself; she committed suicide. *Personality:* mistrustful; gullible. **Page 39.**

DEMETER (de-**meet**-a) *Roman:* Ceres. *Category:* goddess. *Family Status:* d. of Cronos and Rhea; two s. and two d. incl. Persephone (fa. Zeus). *Career:* goddess of the Earth and harvests; responsible for growth and fertility of fruit and crops; helped by Persephone; driven to desperation when Persephone seized by Pluto; abandoned her duties to search for her; after intervention by Zeus, had to accept a compromise – Persephone would spend half the year with her and half with Pluto; when Persephone is away, Demeter mourns and it is winter; accidentally ate shoulder of Pelops when served up to the gods for dinner by Tantalus. *Personality:*

strong maternal instinct, to the point of neglecting her duty; generous and bountiful. *Distinguishing Features:* often shown holding corn. *Supernatural·Attributes:* immortality. **Page 11.**

DEUCALION (dew-**kale**-ee-on) *Category:* demi-god. *Family Status:* s. of Prometheus; m. Pyrrha; ancestor of whole human race. *Career:* warned by Prometheus when Zeus was about to flood the world and drown all mortals; survived by building a boat; when water subsided, obeyed the command of Zeus's messenger to throw stones over his shoulder – these became men; Pyrrha threw stones which became women, so human race began again. *Personality:* a good man; strong survival instinct. **Page 21.**

DIANA see **ARTEMIS.**

DIDO see **AENEAS.**

DIOMEDES (die-om-**ee**-deez) i. *Category:* mortal. *Career:* hero; fought for Greeks in Trojan War; wounded Aeneas; had the nerve to hurt Aphrodite when she came to Aeneas's rescue. *Personality:* daring – even foolhardy. **Page 42.**

DIOMEDES ii. *Category:* mortal. *Family Status:* s. of Ares and Cyrene. *Career:* king; owner of extremely vicious mares Heracles had to tame as one of his Twelve Labours; eaten by his horses. **Page 38.**

DIONYSUS (die-on-**eye**-sus) *Roman:* Bacchus. *Category:* god. *Family Status:* s. of Zeus and Semele; born from Zeus's thigh, where he was kept safe until his birth, after Semele was killed; m. Ariadne; six s. *Career:* god of wine and the theatre; travelled round teaching people how to make wine from grapes; led a life of pleasure; attracted fanatical followers, especially women, called Maenads; mystery cult formed to worship him; associated with drunkenness and licentious behaviour; deliberately provoked murder of Pentheus. *Personality:* fun-loving; womanizing; wild. *Distinguishing Features:* dark, curly hair, red lips, sparkling eyes; carries the thyrsos, a stick entwined with vine leaves; keeps undesirable company, such as Silenus and the satyrs. *Supernatural Attributes:* immortality; grants followers the power to tear animals (and people) limb from limb, bare-handed. **Pages 18. 19.**

DORUS (**door**-us) see **HELLEN.**

DRYADS (**dry**-adds) *Category:* demi-goddesses; tree-nymphs. *Personalities:* generally gentle and good. *Distinguishing Features:* beautiful; their life was linked to that of their tree. *Supernatural Attributes:* long life.

EAST WIND see **EURUS.**

ECHIDNE (ek-**kid**-nee) *Category:* monster. *Family Status:* six children, Orthrus (Geryon's dog), Cerberus, Hydra, Chimaera (fa. Typhon); Sphinx, Nemean Lion (fa. Orthrus). *Distinguishing Features:* half-woman, half-serpent. *Supernatural Attributes:* giving birth to monsters.

ECHO (**ekk**-o) *Category:* demi-goddess; nymph. *Family Status:* would-be lo. of Narcissus. *Career:* offended Hera and was condemned to repeat last few words that anyone said to her; fell in love with Narcissus but was rejected by him; pined away until only her voice was left. *Personality:* indiscreet; mournful and lonely. *Distinguishing Features:* unable to say anything of her own; invisible once she had faded away. *Supernatural Attributes:* long life. *Associations:* the way your words repeat if you shout them in the mountains or a tunnel is called an "echo". **Page 30.**

ELECTRA (ee-**lect**-ra) *Category:* mortal. *Family Status:* d. of Agamemnon and Clytemnestra; m. Pylades. *Career:* princess; badly affected by murder of her father by her mother; accessory to murder of her mother, by encouraging her brother, Orestes, to take revenge. *Personality:* vengeful; unforgiving. **Page 44.**

ENDYMION (en-**dim**-ee-on) *Category:* mortal. *Career:* fell in love with Selene; languished and dreamt about Selene; wished he need do nothing else; achieved a sort of immortality when his wish was granted by Zeus and she put him into eternal sleep in which he never grew old. *Personality:* romantic, dreamy. *Distinguishing Features:* in permanent sleep. *Supernatural Attributes:* eternally young. **Page 17.**

EOS (**ee**-oss) *Roman:* Aurora. ·*Category:* goddess. *Family Status:* d. of Hyperion and the Titaness, Theia; lo. of Orion. *Career:* goddess of the dawn; responsible for the rising of the sun each morning; drove a chariot; cursed by Aphrodite to fall for lots of young men, after she had an affair with Ares; was slighted by Orion, who abandoned her to go hunting with Artemis. *Personality:* fond of men. *Distinguishing Features:* thought of as coloured liked the dawn sky – rosy-fingered, saffron-robed. *Supernatural Attributes:* immortality. **Page 29.**

EPIMETHEUS (epp-ee-**mee**-thyoos) *Category:* Titan. *Family Status:* brother to Prometheus; one d. Pyrrha. *Career:* rather ineffectually helped his brother with the creation of mankind; he welcomed Pandora, though he had been warned not to accept gifts from Zeus, and thereby hastened the introduction of evil into the world by Pandora's curiosity; his name means "afterthought." *Personality:* easily taken in; susceptible to a pretty girl. *Supernatural Attributes:* immortality. **Page 21.**

ERINYES (air-**in**-yeez) *Category:* demi-goddesses. *Family Status:* sprang from Uranus's blood. *Career:* appointed by the gods to trouble the conscience of murderers, especially those who murder rela-

Erinye

tives. *Personalities:* persistent; terrifying to the guilty – no trouble at all to the innocent. *Distinguishing Features:* three of them; normally considered to be female; when in pursuit, they have a dog's head, snakes for hair and bats' wings. *Supernatural Attributes:* immortality; ability to inflict mental torture on victims. *Associations:* euphemistically called Eumenides (Kindly Ones). **Pages 8, 45.**

ERIS (**air**-iss) *Category:* goddess. *Family Status:* d. of Zeus and Hera; twin to Ares. *Career:* goddess of spite; cause of the Trojan War by bringing golden apple inscribed "For the fairest" to wedding feast of Thetis and Peleus. *Personality:* spiteful; trouble-making; revengeful. *Supernatural Attributes:* immortality.

EROS (**ear**-oss) *Roman:* Cupid. *Category:* god. *Family Status:* not clear; sometimes said to be s. of Ares and Aphrodite; m. Psyche. *Career:* specialized in making people fall in love – even unsuitable couples;

Eros

fell in love with Psyche when grazed with his own arrow; became her lo. in secret; when the secret was disclosed, Aphrodite was furious and Eros was forbidden to see Psyche; Zeus was touched by Eros and Psyche's joint efforts to gain the forgiveness of Aphrodite and made Psyche immortal so they could marry and live together on Olympus. *Personality:* mischievous; fond of romantic intrigues. *Distinguishing Features:* young and handsome; charming; carried gold bow and arrows, used to make people fall in love; has wings. *Supernatural Attributes:* immortality; irresistible love-inducing ability. **Pages 13, 31.**

EUMENIDES (you-**men**-ee-deez) see **ERINYES.**

EURIPIDES (you-**rip**-ee-deez) Real person, who wrote plays using stories from myths. Lived from 480-406 BC.

EUROPA (you-**rope**-a) *Category:* mortal. *Family Status:* sister of Cadmus; lo. of Zeus; three s. Minos, Rhadamanthys, Sarpedon (fa. Zeus); m. King of Crete. *Career:* carefree childhood until carried off by Zeus in the form of a white bull; taken to Crete, where she had his three sons; later m. the king and got him to accept Minos as heir to the throne. *Personality:* naive, loving. **Page 22.**

EURUS (**your**-us) *Category:* god. *Family Status:* kept by Aeolus in a bag. *Career:* East Wind; blew as the gods directed. *Personality:* violent and disorderly. *Distinguishing Features:* sometimes given a serpent's tail. *Supernatural Attributes:* immortality; creating storms.

EURYDICE (you-**rid**-ee-see) *Category:* demi-goddess; dryad. *Family Status:* m. Orpheus. *Career:* happy as Orpheus's wife until bothered by the attentions of

Aristaeus; running from him, she received a lethal snake-bite; Orpheus followed her to the Underworld to beg Pluto to let her go; he succeeded, but broke conditions of her release by turning to look at her before she had left the gates of the Underworld; they were re-united after Orpheus's death. *Personality:* faithful, sad. **Page 31.**

EURYSTHEUS (you-**riss**-thyoos) *Category:* mortal. *Career:* king; chosen by the Oracle as the man to set the Twelve Labours for Heracles; he suffered the consequences, as Heracles brought terrifying live trophies to show him. *Personality:* rather cowardly; not a man of action. **Page 37.**

FURIES (**fyoor**-eez) see **ERINYES.**

GALATEA (gal-at-**tay**-a) *Category:* became mortal. *Family Status:* m. Pygmalion. *Career:* was created as a statue by Pygmalion; he fell in love with her; Aphrodite was moved by his love for her and brought her to life; they lived happily ever after. *Personality:* loving and dutiful. *Distinguishing Features:* statuesque. **Page 13.**

GANYMEDE (**gan**-ee-meed) *Category:* mortal, becoming immortal. *Family Status:* s. of King Tros; loved by Eos and Zeus. *Career:* was snatched up to Olympus by an eagle sent by Zeus; took over from Hebe as cup-bearer to the gods. *Personality:* attractive; athletic. *Distinguishing Features:* extremely handsome. *Supernatural Attributes:* immortality, once he was taken to Olympus. *Associations:* his image set in the stars as Aquarius, the water-carrier. **Page 48.**

GERYON (gair-**eye**-on) *Category:* giant. *Career:* owner and guardian of marvellous cattle; killed by Heracles, who had to capture the cattle for one of his Twelve Labours. *Personality:* aggressive in defence of his property. *Distinguishing Features:* three bodies above the waist. *Supernatural Attributes:* enormous size; triple weapon-wielding ability. **Page 38.**

GLAUCIS (**glaw**-sis) *Category:* mortal. *Family Status:* was to m. Jason. *Career:* innocently intending to become Jason's wife, when she suffered a horrible death; on the eve of the wedding, Medea gave her a dress and crown as presents, which burst into flames when she put them on. *Personality:* blameless victim. **Page 33.**

GLAUCUS (**glaw**-kuss) *Category:* mortal. *Family Status:* one s. Bellerophon. *Career:* king; offended Aphrodite, who fed his horses magic herbs and water from her well on the eve of a chariot race so they bolted and killed him. *Personality:* rather reckless. **Page 13.**

GOLDEN RACE: *Category:* mortal. *Family Status:* created by Zeus; no children. *Career:* created to live on Earth; blissful existence in peaceful world; shortlived, as the whole race died out through not having children; their spirits lingered on in tranquil places and helped and protected later races. *Personality:* good, peaceable, beneficient. *Super-*

natural Attributes: their protective spirits can be sensed by humans. **Page 20.**

GORGONS (gore-gonz) *Category:* monsters. *Family Status:* three d. of Phorcys – two immortal, one mortal. *Career:* once beautiful, were turned into hideous monsters for offending Athene; turned anyone who looked at them to stone; one of them,

Gorgon

Medusa, was killed by Perseus. *Personalities:* evil, destructive. *Distinguishing Features:* wings, bronze claws, serpents for hair; their lair could be easily recognized by worn statues of victims. *Supernatural Attributes:* turning people to stone. **Page 24.**

HADES (**hay**-deez) Another name for Pluto, god of the Underworld, or for the Underworld itself. See **PLUTO.**

HAEMON (**he**-mon) *Category:* mortal. *Family Status:* s. of Creon; lo. of Antigone. *Career:* prince; Antigone hanged herself after his father condemned her to death for finding and burying her brother who was killed in battle; killed himself. *Personality:* brave and defiant. **Page 48.**

HARMONIA (har-**moan**-ee-a) *Category:* goddess. *Family Status:* d. of Aphrodite and Ares; m. Cadmus. *Career:* bringing back peace after war to prepare the way for her mother, the goddess of love, to return; went to Isles of the Blessed when she died. *Personality:* diplomatic, tactful. *Supernatural Attributes:* immortality. **Page 13.**

HARPIES (har-peez) *Category:* monsters. *Career:* taking victims to Erinyes for punishment; pestering human victims by stealing their food and screeching so they cannot sleep; harried King Phineas until

Harpy

driven from his court by Jason and the Argonauts. *Personality:* nasty; persistent and tireless; extremely unwelcome visitors. *Distinguishing Features:* birds with nagging, female heads. *Supernatural Attributes:* flying and nagging abilities in deadly combination. **Page 32.**

HEBE (**hee**-bee) *Category:* goddess. *Family Status:* d. of Zeus and Hera; sometimes said to have married Heracles when he became immortal. *Career:* cup-bearer to the gods; made redundant by Ganymede who took the job when brought to Olympus by Zeus. *Personality:* obliging and helpful. *Distinguishing Features:* often carries a jug of nectar. *Supernatural Attributes:* immortality. **Page 48.**

HECTOR (**heck**-tor) *Category:* mortal. *Family Status:* s. of King Priam and Queen Hecuba of Troy; m. Andromache. *Career:* professional warrior; great hero for Troy in Trojan War; killed Patroclus; humiliated in death when killed by furious Achilles and dragged round the walls of Troy behind his chariot; Trojans had to pay to get his body for burial. *Personality:* noble and brave; good leader. **Page 42.**

HECUBA (**heck**-you-ba) *Category:* mortal. *Family Status:* m. King Priam of Troy; children incl. Hector, Paris, Cassandra. *Career:* queen. **Page 40.**

HELEN (**hell**-en) *Category:* demi-goddess. *Family Status:* d. of Zeus and Leda; m. Menelaus; one d. Hermione; lo. of Paris. *Career:* abducted by Theseus as a child but rescued by her brothers, Castor and Polydeuces; obediently married according to her step-father, Tyndareus's, wishes; caught up in divine plotting when Aphrodite promised Paris would have her in return for choosing herself as the loveliest goddess; she fell in love with Paris and ran away with him, which started the Trojan War; surprisingly, she was taken back by Menelaus at the end of the war; taken to Olympus by Zeus; became goddess of sailors. *Personality:* much desired by men; she sometimes hated herself for the trouble her beauty caused. *Distinguishing Features:* the most beautiful woman in the world. *Associations:* hers was "the face which launched a thousand ships" (meaning the fleet that sailed to Troy), in "Doctor Faustus" by Christopher Marlowe. **Page 41.**

HELIOS (**hee**-lee-oss) *Category:* Titan. *Family Status:* descended from Uranus and Mother Earth; one s. Phaeton. *Career:* keeper of sacred cattle; drove chariot of the sun across the sky each day; foolishly allowed Phaeton to have a go at the reins; Phaeton's reckless driving endangered the Earth and he was killed by Zeus. *Personality:* over-indulgent father. *Distinguishing Features:* golden, shining, like the sun. *Supernatural Attributes:* immortality. *Associations:* his name has been used for things associated with the sun e.g. the flower, heliotrope, which turns to follow the sun and the gas, Helium, first discovered among gases surrounding the sun. **Page 26.**

HELLE (**hell**-a) *Category:* mortal. *Family Status:* d. of Athamas and Nephele, the cloud-woman. *Career:* unreasonably hated by her step-mother, Ino; escaped with her brother, Phrixus, on back of golden ram sent by Hera; she fell from the ram's back into the sea as it crossed from Europe to Asia. *Personality:* innocent victim. *Associations:* the strip of water where Europe (Greece) meets Asia (Turkey) was named the Hellespont (Sea of Helle) after her. **Page 25.**

HELLEN (**hell**-en) *Category:* demi-god. *Family Status:* s. of Deucalion; grands. of Prometheus; s. incl. Aeolus, Dorus; grands. include Ion, Achaeus. *Career:* legendary founder of four so-called Hellenic races – Aeolians, Dorians, Ionians and Achaeans. *Personality:* noble; dynasty-building. *Associations:* the Greeks still call their country Hellas. **Page 48.**

HEPHAESTOS (heff-**eest**-oss) *Roman:* Vulcan. *Category:* god. *Family Status:* s. of Hera alone; m. Aphrodite. *Career:* rather hard-done-by; born lame; thrown from Olympus in a rage by Hera and crippled; m. Aphrodite at Zeus's command, against her will – suffered her infidelities; employed as smith in the gods' forge; skilled craftsman, called upon to make armour and jewels for the gods; respected and admired for his work in the end. *Personality:* tends to keep in the background; even-tempered except when especially roused to jealousy by Aphrodite; hardworking; good with his hands; beneficient, kindly; *Distinguishing Features:* strong but coarse; dark, deformed; usually to be found in his forge, with tools of his trade. *Supernatural Attributes:* immortality; crafting super-protective weapons for special purposes. **Page 12.**

HERA (**hair**-a) *Roman:* Juno. *Category:* goddess. *Family Status:* d. of Cronos and Rhea; m. her brother, Zeus; two s. Ares (fa. Zeus), Hephaestos (no father); two d. Eris, Hebe (fa. Zeus). *Career:* Queen of the gods and protectress of women but spent a lot of time pursuing Zeus's lovers and devising punishments for them; rivalry between herself, Athene and Aphrodite; supported Greeks in Trojan War because she held a grudge against Paris, for choosing Aphrodite as the most beautiful goddess; little evidence of any kindly feelings towards mortals; especially made Heracles's life a misery. *Personality:* haughty; jealous; vain; sometimes cruel. *Distinguishing Features:* one of the most beautiful goddesses; famed for her white arms – a sign of beauty. *Supernatural Attributes:* immortality; can inflict madness. *Associations:* the peacock was her symbol – she set the eyes of her 100-eyed servant, Argus, in its tail. **Pages 9, 11.**

HERACLES (**hair**-a-kleez) *Roman:* Hercules. *Category:* demi-god. *Family Status:* s. of Zeus and Alcmene; m. Megara; m. Deianeira; several children with both wives; sometimes said to have married Hebe when made immortal. *Career:* adventuring; Argonaut; fighting monsters; unfairly hounded by Hera, who was jealous of Zeus's affair with his mother; was driven temporarily mad by Hera and killed his first wife and children; although it was not his fault, he had to make amends for their deaths; consulted the Oracle and was told to perform Twelve Labours (impossible tasks) set by King Eurystheus; managed them all successfully – mostly feats of strength; purged his guilt and he re-married; premature death when tricked into wearing a poisoned shirt given to him innocently by Deianeira; he could not take it off, nor bear the pain, so he built a pyre and climbed on it to die; Zeus rescued him and took him to Olympus to be an Immortal; left his bow to Philoctetes. *Personality:* exceptionally strong and brave; man of action, not thought. *Distinguishing Features:* hugely-built and powerful; wore extra-tough skin from Nemean lion as a cape for protection. *Supernatural Attributes:* super-human strength; immortality, once taken to Olympus by Zeus. **Pages 37, 38, 39.**

HERMES (**her**-meez) *Roman:* Mercury. *Category:* god. *Family Status:* s. of Zeus and Titaness Maia. *Career:* precocious and naughty as a child; stole Apollo's cattle; won Apollo's forgiveness by inventing lyre and giving it to

Hermes

him; given job as messenger of the gods, carrying Zeus's commands, to keep him out of trouble; was also the god of thieves because of stealing Apollo's cattle and of treaties because of his diplomatic way of calming Apollo; said to have invented the alphabet, boxing and gymnastics. *Personality:* quick-witted; energetic; somewhat mischievous, even a thief; excellent at bargaining to his own advantage; inventive. *Distinguishing Features:* winged helmet and sandals. *Supernatural Attributes:* speedy flight for delivering messages; immortality. *Associations:* Roman name given to the substance Mercury because it moves so quickly when in liquid metal form. **Page 19.**

HERMIONE (her-**my**-on-nee) *Category:* mortal. *Family Status:* d. of Menelaus and Helen; m. Orestes.

HESIONE (hess-**eye**-on-ee) see **PRIAM.**

HESPERIDES (hess-**pair**-ee-deez) *Category:* demi-goddesses. *Family Status:* d. of Atlas and Hesperis. *Career:* gardeners; looked after Hera's golden apples of immortality; allowed Atlas to take some to give to Heracles for one of his Twelve Labours; sweet singers. *Personalities:* patient; kindly. *Supernatural Attributes:* immortality. **Page 39.**

HESTIA (**hess**-tee-a) *Roman:* Vesta. *Category:* goddess. *Family Status:* d. of Cronos and Rhea. *Career:* protectress of the hearth; she was very popular – protected homes and was well-loved; did not get involved much in adventures and fights; gave up her place on Olympus to Dionysus. *Personality:* protective; gentle; kind. *Distinguishing Features:* virgin goddess. *Supernatural Attributes:* immortality; powerful protecting ability.

HIPPODAMIA (hip-o-dam-**me**-a) *Category:* mortal. *Family Status:* d. of King Oenomaus; m. Pelops; many children incl. Atreus. *Career:* princess; swept off her feet by Pelops and married him, although he killed her father in a chariot race; *Personality:* romantically reckless. **Page 49.**

HIPPOLYTE (hip-**pol**-ee-tee) *Category:* mortal. *Family Status:* m. Theseus; one s. Hippolytus. *Career:* warrior Queen of the Amazons; would have given her girdle (belt) freely to Heracles when he had to fetch it as one of his Twelve Labours, but Hera caused the Amazons to attack him so he had to fight for it; fought at Theseus's side and died in battle. *Personality:* fierce, *Distinguishing Features:* tall and strong; favoured warrior dress. **Pages 36, 38.**

HIPPOLYTUS (hip-**poll**-it-us) *Category:*

mortal. *Family Status:* s. of Theseus and Hippolyte. *Career:* unfortunate victim of his stepmother, Phaedra; she claimed he had attacked her; Theseus prayed to Poseidon to punish his son; Poseidon sent a great wave to kill him, although he was innocent. *Personality:* honourable; honest. **Page 25.**

HOMER (**home**-er) Real man. Supposed author of The Iliad, The Odyssey.

HYACINTHUS (hi-a-**sinth**-us) *Category:* mortal. *Career:* Spartan prince; he was favoured by the gods and became special friend of Apollo; the West Wind was jealous and plotted his downfall – blew a discus thrown by

Hyacinth

Hyacinthus back in his face and killed him. *Personality:* carefree; pleasure-seeking. *Distinguishing Features:* very handsome; athletic. *Associations:* where his blood fell the first hyacinth flowers grew. **Page 48.**

HYPERION (hi-**peer**-ee-on) *Category:* Titan. *Family Status:* s. of Uranus and Mother Earth; one s. Helios; two d. Eos (the dawn) and Selene (the moon). *Career:* sun-god – eclipsed by Apollo when New Gods took over from Titans. *Distinguishing Features:* bright, shining, golden. *Supernatural Attributes:* immortality.

ICARUS (**ick**-er-us) *Category:* mortal. *Family Status:* s. of Daedalus. *Career:* high-flying but brief; imprisoned with his father when Daedalus displeased Minos; escaped on wings of wax and feathers made by Daedalus; got carried away by being able to fly, went too close to the sun which melted the wax and the wings disintegrated; fell into the sea and was killed. *Personality:* arrogant, ambitious. *Associations:* the sea where he fell to his death is called Icarian after him. **Page 26.**

INO (**ee**-no) *Category:* mortal. *Family Status:* d. of Cadmus; m. Athamas; two s. *Career:* desperate for her own son to be heir to the throne, she wanted to dispose of her step-children, Phrixus and Helle; hatched devious plan to make Athamas think he must sacrifice his son; foiled by Hera, who got Hermes to send golden ram to rescue the children. *Personality:* many unpleasant characteristics – jealous, selfish, cruel and cunning. **Page 25.**

IO (**ee**-oh) *Category:* mortal. *Family Status:* d. of river-god, Inachus; lo. of Zeus. *Career:* priestess of Hera; attracted Zeus's attention and he turned her into a cow to keep the affair from Hera; Hera tied the cow up and placed Argus to guard her; Hermes released her but Hera sent a gadfly to sting her non-stop; she ran to Egypt where she became a woman again and a priestess of the Egyptian goddess, Isis. *Personality:* mild, loving. *Distinguishing Features:* beautiful; took the form of a gentle white cow during her transformation. **Page 22.**

ION (ee-on) see **HELLEN.**

IPHIGENIA (if-ij-a-**nee**-a) *Category:* mortal. *Family Status:* d. of Agamemnon and Clytemnestra. *Career:* on the point of being sacrificed by her father to gain a good wind to sail to Troy, was saved by Artemis, who put a deer in her place; assumed dead, but actually became priestess of Artemis among the Taurians; she rescued her brother, Orestes, when he was about to be sacrificed by the Taurians for stealing their statue of Artemis; never married. *Personality:* rather serious; dedicated priestess. **Page 17.**

IRIS (**eye**-riss) *Category:* goddess. *Career:* goddess of the rainbow and messenger of Hera. *Personality:* obedient; quiet *Supernatural Attributes:* immortality.

IXION (**icks**-ee-on) *Category:* mortal. *Career:* King of the Lapiths; nasty piece of work; murdered his future father-in-law; planned to steal Hera from Zeus; Zeus made Nephele out of clouds as Hera's double, to test Ixion; he fell for the trick and attempted to grab her; his guilt was thus proved and Zeus had him tied to a wheel of fire which was sent rolling across the heavens fogever. *Personality:* arrogant, presumptuous; defiant of the gods. **Page 26.**

JASON (**jace**-on) *Category:* mortal. *Family Status:* nephew of Pelias. *Career:* cheated of his inheritance to the throne of Iolcus by Pelias; grew up in exile; returned to claim his throne – was told he could be heir if he brought golden fleece from Colchis; set out in a ship (Argo), with many heroes (Argonauts); had many adventures; was helped by Medea to steal the fleece from its dragon-serpent guard; returned to Iolcus with Medea; she caused death of Pelias so the people banished her and Jason; he became King of Corinth; decided to abandon Medea to marry Princess Glauce; Medea caused Glauce's death and the Corinthians banished them too; ended his life an outcast; was sitting under the rotting remains of the Argo when prow fell and killed him. *Personality:* heroic, ambitious; became too proud and greedy for power; hurt those who loved him. *Supernatural Attributes:* had special help from the gods (Hera and Aphrodite made Medea fall in love with him and help him) before he lost their favour by his behaviour. **Pages 32, 33.**

JOCASTA (jock-**ass**-ta) *Category:* mortal. *Family Status:* m. Laius; one s. Oedipus; m. Oedipus; two s. and two d. (fa. Oedipus). *Career:* Queen of Thebes; destined for a terrible Fate; was told by Oracle that her son would murder his father and marry his mother, so abandoned Oedipus to die; he survived, unknowingly killed his father in a roadside dispute and later came to Thebes as a hero for killing the Sphinx; his reward was to marry Jocasta and become king; this fulfilled the prophesy; when the truth was revealed, she hanged herself in shame. *Personality:* high-principled; respectful; good. **Page 29.**

LAIUS (**lay**-us) *Category:* mortal. *Family Status:* m. Jocasta; one s. Oedipus. *Career:* King of Thebes; fell foul of Oracle which predicted he would be killed by his own son; despite efforts to avoid it by exposing Oedipus to die, the baby survived and Laius met him (without recognizing him) when he grew up and quarrelled with him over who should give way on a road; they fought and Oedipus killed him, so the prophecy came true. See also **JOCASTA** and **OEDIPUS.** *Personality:* stubborn, unlucky. **Page 29.**

LEDA (**leed**-a) *Category:* mortal. *Family Status:* m. King Tyndareus of Sparta; lo. of Zeus; two s. Castor (fa. Tyndareus), Polydeuces (fa. Zeus); two d. Clytemnestra (fa. Tyndareus), Helen (fa. Zeus). *Career:* Queen of Sparta; seduced by Zeus disguised as a swan – their daughter, Helen, was the most beautiful woman in the world and the outward cause of the Trojan War. *Personality:* straightforward, good. *Distinguishing Features:* beautiful enough to catch Zeus's eye. **Page 23.**

LERNEAN HYDRA (lern-**ee**-an **hi**-dra) *Category:* monster. *Career:* death and destruction; terrorized swamps of Lerna; killed by Heracles as one of his Twelve Labours. *Personality:* vicious; not keen on humans. *Distinguishing Features:* dog-like body; many serpent's heads. *Supernatural Attributes:* heads grow again when cut off – this can only be prevented by sealing the severed neck with fire. **Page 37.**

Hydra

LETO (**lee**-toe) *Category:* Titaness. *Family Status:* lo. of Zeus; one s. Apollo (fa. Zeus); one d. Artemis (fa. Zeus). *Career:* had affair with Zeus; was persecuted by Hera, who set her giant snake, Python, on Leto out of jealousy; the South Wind helped by carrying her to Ortygia, where Artemis was born; Artemis helped her to Delos, where Apollo was born; rewarded by the fierce protection of her twin children. *Personality:* brave, long-suffering. *Supernatural Attributes:* immortality. *Associations:* quail was her bird. **Page 16.**

LOTUS-EATERS (**low**-tuss eaters) *Category:* mortals. *Career:* eating lotus-fruit; these caused people to forget everything except wanting to eat more of the flowers. *Personalities:* robbed of personality by poisonous effect

Lotus

of the flowers, which erased all memories. *Distinguishing Features:* only to be found in Libya, where lotus-flowers grew; permanently in a dream-like trance. **Page 46.**

MAENADS (**meen**-adds) *Roman:* Bacchantes. *Category:* mortals. *Career:*

women followers of Dionysus; infamous for frenzied behaviour and wild dancing during their ceremonies. See **AGAVE, PENTHEUS**. *Personalities:* normal, until under the influence of Dionysian rites, when they could become violent if disturbed. *Distinguishing Features:* female; wear fawn-skins; carry thyrsos, stick wrapped with ivy. *Supernatural Attributes:* superhuman strength when in religious trance – could tear animals to pieces with their bare hands. **Page 19.**

MAIA (my-a) *Category:* Titaness. *Family Status:* d. of Atlas; lo. of Zeus; one s. Hermes (fa. Zeus). *Career:* surprisingly peaceful, unlike most of Zeus's lovers. *Supernatural Attributes:* immortality.

MARSYAS (mar-see-ass) *Category:* demigod; satyr. *Career:* usual satyr-like preoccupations – chasing nymphs, getting drunk with Dionysus, enjoying himself; found the cursed flute Athene threw away; foolishly challenged Apollo to a music contest in which the loser was to be killed; he lost and Apollo skinned him alive. *Personality:* pleasure-seeking; womanizing; lack of respect for the gods. *Distinguishing Features:* horse's ears and tail. **Page 16.**

MEDEA (med-dee-a) *Category:* mortal. *Family Status:* d. of King Aeetes; lo. of Jason; m. Aegeus; one s.. *Career:* professional enchantress; fell in love with Jason when he came to seek the golden fleece; betrayed her father to help him, then escaped with him; killed her half-brother; tricked Pelias's daughters into killing Pelias; caused herself and Jason to be banished from Iolcus; was heiress to throne of Corinth, so went there and made Jason king; furious when Jason decided to marry Princess Glauce – sent her a poisoned dress and crown as "gifts", which killed her when she put them on; fled from Corinth; sometimes accused of killing her children first, though it may have been the Corinthians who did it; tried to poison Theseus while m. to Aegeus; cured Heracles of his madness; she became an Immortal and ruled the Elysian Fields; some say she m. Achilles in the Underworld. *Personality:* extreme; passionate. *Distinguishing Features:* drove a chariot pulled by dragon-serpents. *Supernatural Attributes:* skilled in making magic potions. **Pages 32, 33.**

MEDUSA (med-yoos-a) *Category:* monster; Gorgon. *Family Status:* d. of sea-god, Phorcys; Pegasus sprang from her blood. *Career:* she offended Athene, who turned her and her sisters into monsters; from then on, turning humans to stone became her main pastime; was killed by Perseus, with the help of weapons from the gods. *Personality:* vindictive; impersonal hatred of all humans. *Distinguishing Features:* protruding tongue, bulging eyes, serpents instead of hair, wings, bronze claws; her home can be recognized by crumbling statues of humans surrounding it. *Supernatural Attributes:* able to petrify people. **Page 24.**

MEGARA (meg-er-a) see **HERACLES**.

MENELAUS (men-a-lay-us) *Category:* mortal. *Family Status:* brother of Agamemnon; m. Helen; one d. Hermione. *Career:* King of Sparta; chosen as Helen's husband from all the Greek princes; sadly, she did not love him; when she was abducted by Paris, Menelaus and Agamemnon raised a force against Troy and embarked on the Trojan War; after the war, he found he still loved Helen and took her back. *Personality:* rough and ready; brave but not too bright. *Distinguishing Features:* good at making loud war-cry. **Pages 41, 43.**

METIS (meet-iss) *Category:* Titaness. *Family Status:* lo. of Zeus. *Career:* Titaness of wisdom; advised Zeus; she was expecting Zeus's child when it was predicted that if she had a son, he would be greater than his father, so Zeus turned her into a fly and swallowed her; he later developed a headache, had his skull broken open and out came Athene. *Personality:* very clever and wise. *Supernatural Attributes:* her wisdom lived on through Athene. **Page 14.**

MIDAS (my-dass) *Category:* mortal. *Family Status:* one d. *Career:* helped Silenus when drunk and earned reward from Dionysus; wished that everything he touched should turn to gold; soon his palace, his food and even his d. had turned to gold and he was starving and lonely; the wish was undone; offended Apollo and was given ass's ears as punishment; hid them under his cap, but his barber saw them and word got out that Midas had been punished for his foolishness. *Personality:* thoughtless; greedy for riches; rather stupid; obstinate. *Supernatural Attributes:* ability to turn things to gold during the time Dionysus granted his wish. **Page 27.**

MINERVA (min-urv-a) see **ATHENE**.

MINOS (my-noss) *Category:* mortal. *Family Status:* s. of Zeus and Europa; m. Pasiphae; one s. Androgeus; two d. Ariadne, Phaedra. *Career:* powerful king of Crete; successful warrior – defeated Nisus with the help of his treacherous daughter, Scylla; guardian of the Minotaur; demanded hostages from the mainland to feed to the Minotaur in compensation for the death of his son, whom the Greeks had killed; betrayed by Ariadne when she helped Theseus kill the Minotaur, then escaped with him; became a judge of the dead when he died. *Personality:* strong but harsh and not well-loved by his daughter or wife. **Pages 34, 36, 48.**

MINOTAUR (my-no-tore) *Category:* monster. *Family Status:* s. of Poseidon's bull and Pasiphae. *Career:* lived in Labyrinth designed by Daedalus; ate human flesh; killed by Theseus. *Personality:* evil, murderous, full of hatred. *Distinguishing Features:* head and shoulders of a bull, body of a man. *Supernatural Attributes:* fantastic strength and devouring ability. **Pages 34, 36.**

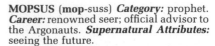
Minotaur

MOPSUS (mop-suss) *Category:* prophet. *Career:* renowned seer; official advisor to the Argonauts. *Supernatural Attributes:* seeing the future.

MOTHER EARTH *Category:* goddess. *Family Status:* emerged into existence from Chaos; one s. Uranus; m. Uranus; many children – plants and animals, the Cyclopes, strange-shaped giants and monsters, the Titans. *Career:* creating the Earth and giving birth to creatures that populate it; developed hatred for Uranus and successfully encouraged her son, Cronos, to rebel against him; answered Daphne's prayer when she was fleeing from Apollo, by turning her into a laurel tree; angered by Orion saying he could kill all monsters, as they were all her children. *Personality:* motherly; protective; gets angry if her children are mistreated. *Distinguishing Features:* she is the Earth. *Supernatural Attributes:* giving birth to supernatural beings; immortality. *Associations:* also called Ge or Gaia. **Pages 8, 29.**

MUSES (myooz-iz) *Category:* demigoddesses. *Family Status:* nine d. of Zeus and Mnemosyne (memory). *Career:* inspiring creativity in artists and scientists; originally lived wild on Mount Parnassus but were tamed by Apollo and became his companions. *Personalities:* creative; artistic; elusive. *Distinguishing Features:* beautiful young women. *Supernatural Attributes:* immortality; able to inspire intellectual endeavour. **Page 16.**

MYRTILUS (mer-till-uss) *Category:* mortal. *Career:* charioteer to King Oenomaus; sabotaged the king's chariot before the race with Pelops, so it crashed; Oenomaus was killed and Pelops could marry his daughter, Hippodamia; his thanks from Pelops was to be thrown out of his chariot while they were escaping; he drowned. *Personality:* not to be trusted; disloyal; selfish. *Associations:* linked with myrtle, Aphrodite's flower. **Page 49.**

NAIADS (nye-adds) *Category:* demigoddesses. *Career:* they were spirits of nature who lived in streams and waterfalls; often attended a god or goddess; could harm mortals but did not often do so. *Personalities:* generally happy and kind. *Distinguishing Features:* pretty young maidens; to be found near fresh water sources. *Supernatural Attributes:* long life.

NARCISSUS (nar-sis-us) *Category:* mortal. *Career:* concern for his own beauty; hurting anyone who fell in love with him by his indifference and egotism; caused Echo to fade away to nothing for unrequited love; punished by Artemis, who made him fall in love with his own reflection; committed suicide when he realized he would never love anyone better than himself. *Personality:* exceedingly vain; callous; insensi-

Narcissus

tive to others. *Distinguishing Features:* excessive good looks. *Associations:* gave his name to flower, narcissus; self-love can be called "narcissism". **Page 30.**

NEMESIS (nem-a-sis) *Category:* goddess. *Career:* she brought retribution (just punishment) to people who did wrong; especially punished presumptuousness towards the gods. *Personality:* remorseless; unavoidable. *Supernatural Attributes:* immortality.

NEOPTOLEMUS (nee-op-**tol**-ee-muss) *Roman:* Pyrrhus. *Career:* mortal. *Family Status:* s. of Achilles and Deidamia. *Career:* miltary; fought by his father at Troy; inherited Achilles's armour after Ajax and Agamemnon argued over it; entered Troy inside the Wooden Horse; killed Hector's son and carried off Andromache. *Personality:* daring; vengeful; arrogant. **Page 42.**

NEPHELE (neff-ee-lee) *Category:* demi-goddess. *Family Status:* created by Zeus out of clouds; m. Athamas; two s. incl. Phrixus; one d. Helle. *Career:* rather unhappy; made by Zeus to test Ixion – he tried to seize her, proving his wickedness; put aside by Athamas for new wife, Ino; had reason to be much concerned about her children under Ino's care; prayed to Hera to protect them and she answered by sending golden ram to rescue them. *Personality:* insubstantial character; mistreated; fond mother. *Distinguishing Features:* made of clouds in the image of Hera. *Supernatural Attributes:* cannot be caught and held by a mortal because has no solid shape. **Page 26.**

NEREIDS (near-eh-ids) *Category:* demi-goddesses. *Family Status:* d. of Nereus and Doris, sea-deities. *Career:* attending on sea-gods; sometimes involved in mortal lives. *Personalities:* proud, independent. *Distinguishing Features:* their natural form was as beautiful women. *Supernatural Attributes:* could change shape at will, like most sea-deities. See **THETIS. Pages 23, 24.**

NEW GODS The New Gods were **ZEUS, POSEIDON, PLUTO, HESTIA, HERA, DEMETER.**

NIOBE (nye-oh-bee) *Category:* mortal. *Family Status:* sister of Pelops; seven s.; seven d. *Career:* Queen of Thebes; condemned herself when she boasted she was better than Leto as she had seven sons and daughters while Leto had only one of each (Apollo and Artemis); Apollo and Artemis killed all her children except one s. and one d.; she grieved so severely that Zeus took pity and turned her to stone at the peak of Mount Sipylus to stop her suffering. *Personality:* excessive pride in her family leading to boastfulness; foolish lack of respect for the gods; very sad, after the loss of her children. *Distinguishing Features:* turned to stone by Zeus. *Associations:* each year when the snow melted from Mount Sipylus, the water was said to be her tears. **Page 9.**

NISUS (nice-us) *Category:* mortal. *Family Status:* one d. Scylla. *Career:* King of Megara; lost war against Minos by treachery of Scylla who stole his magic lock of hair; killed by Minos; turned into an eagle. *Personality:* aggressive and not very lovable. *Distinguishing Features:* purple lock of hair. *Supernatural Attributes:* possession of magic lock of hair. **Page 25.**

NORTH WIND see **BOREAS**

NYMPHS (nimfs) *Category:* demi-goddesses; see **NAIADS, DRYADS, NEREIDS**. *Career:* spirits of woodland and water; sometimes followers of Dionysus; often chased or loved by mortals or gods; see DAPHNE. *Distinguishing Features:* lovely women; to be found near water, trees or mountains, depending on type. *Supernatural Attributes:* long life.

Nymph

ODYSSEUS (oh-**dee**-see-us) *Roman:* Ulysses. *Category:* mortal. *Family Status:* s. of Laertes; m. Penelope; one s. Telemachus; lo. of Circe; several s. with her. *Career:* reluctant soldier – feigned madness to avoid going to Troy, but made to go in the end; once there, fought bravely; protected Achilles's body after his death; quarrelled with Ajax over Achilles's armour; thought up trick of Wooden Horse; displeased the gods by destructive behaviour after defeat of Troy; suffered mishaps and adventures on his way home – voyages of Odysseus became renowned; he had to throw out the nobles who had taken over his court in his absence; killed by men belonging to his and Circe's son – he had come looking for his father, who thought he was a raider and attacked. *Personality:* home-loving; brave when required; cunning; quick-witted, crafty. *Associations:* Homer's story of his adventures is called The Odyssey. **Pages 46, 47.**

OEDIPUS (ee-dip-puss) *Category:* mortal. *Family Status:* s. of Laius and Jocasta of Thebes; m. Jocasta; several children including d. Antigone. *Career:* bad start – abandoned as a baby to die because of Oracle predicting he would kill his father and marry his mother; he survived, was brought up in court at Corinth; as an adult, met Laius without knowing who he was, quarrelled with him and killed him; answered the riddle of the Sphinx – Thebans gave him the throne and Jocasta for a wife in gratitude; the Oracle was then fulfilled; his real identity revealed by Tiresias, the seer; horrified, Oedipus struck out his eyes and became an outcast, accompanied by Antigone; died near Athens and was buried by Theseus. *Personality:* noble and brave but ill-fated; good ruler; intellectual. *Associations:* Sigmund Freud, called a son's love of his mother and jealousy of his father an "Oedipus complex". **Page 29.**

ORACLE (or-ick-ull) Message from the gods; esp. associated with Apollo at Delphi. **Page 16.**

OREITHYIA (or-**eeth**-yee-a) *Category:* mortal. *Family Status:* d. of King Erechtheus of Athens; m. Boreas, the North Wind; several sons. *Career:* Boreas fell in love with her and carried her off one day while she was out dancing; their sons became Argonauts. *Personality:* good-natured; loving wife. **Page 30.**

ORESTES (or-**rest**-eez) *Category:* mortal. *Family Status:* s. of Agamemnon and Clytemnestra; m. Hermione. *Career:* family cursed by behaviour of ancestors (see **TANTALUS, PELOPS**); brought up away from home; returned after Oracle told him to avenge Agamamnon, who had been murdered by Clytemnestra; urged on by his sister, Electra, he killed Clytemnestra; was tormented by the Erinyes and driven to wandering round Greece; attempted to kill Helen of Troy; demanded trial by the gods – found to have suffered enough, but still tormented by Erinyes; Oracle then sent him to land of Taurians; he was captured and about to be sacrificed but saved by his sister, Iphigenia, presumed dead, but actually a priestess of Artemis among the Taurians; finally, the curse was lifted and he lived normal married life. *Personality:* unwilling hero; prefers quiet life; bad-temper caused by torment from Erinyes. *Distinguishing Features:* accompanied by Erinyes at all times during his atonement. **Pages 44, 45.**

ORION (or-**eye**-on) *Category:* demi-god. *Family Status:* lo. of Eos; lo. of Artemis. *Career:* brilliant hunter; came to sticky end, due to disrespect for goddesses who favoured him; abandoned Eos to hunt with Artemis, thereby annoying Apollo; Mother Earth sent giant scorpion to chase him; Apollo tricked Artemis into shooting him; attempts to have him revived by Asclepius failed; Artemis transformed him into the star-sign Orion. *Personality:* ladies' man; fickle lover; arrogant. *Distinguishing Features:* dashing good looks; hunting gear, especially sword-belt. *Associations:* constellation Orion is still followed across the sky by star-group Scorpio, the scorpion. **Page 29.**

ORPHEUS (or-fee-us) *Category:* mortal. *Family Status:* said to be s. of one of the Muses; m. Eurydice. *Career:* excellent musician on the lyre; accompanied Argonauts; played non-violent but critical role in obtaining golden fleece by playing lullaby to dragon-serpent guard; also prevented loss of ship to the sirens by playing to drown their singing; tragic loss of his wife by snake-bite led him to venture to Underworld to get her back; by playing soothing music, he made a bargain with Pluto and was allowed to take her home, but broke his part of the bargain by looking over his shoulder before Eurydice had left the Underworld and she had to go back; horrible death when torn to shreds by Maenads for refusing to play happy music. *Personality:* artistic, musical; courageous but non-violent; rather sad. *Distinguishing*

Orpheus

Features: always carried his lyre. **Supernatural Attributes:** musical gift from the gods. **Associations:** birds said to sing more sweetly on the spot where he was killed. **Pages 31, 33.**

ORTHRUS (or-**thruss**) **Category:** monster. **Family Status:** s. of Echidne; fa. of Sphinx and Nemean Lion (mo. Echidne). **Career:** guarding cattle of Geryon; killed by Heracles. **Personality:** v. fierce. **Distinguishing Features:** 2-headed dog. **Page 38.**

PALLAS (**pal**-ass) **Category:** demi-goddess. **Family Status:** closely associated with Athene. **Career:** fight-practice partner and friend of Athene; killed accidentally by Athene; Athene called herself Pallas Athene to show her sorrow. **Personality:** noble; a good friend. **Page 15.**

PAN (**pan**) **Roman:** Faunus. **Category:** god. **Family Status:** s. of Hermes; lo. of Syrinx, a nymph. **Career:** god of nature, shepherds, herds and flocks; pursued Syrinx, who escaped him by being turned into a bed of reeds, from which he made pipes to play on; induces panic – unreasonable fear – especially outside or in the country. **Personality:** pleasure-seeking; prone to be over-amorous; frightening if disturbed. **Distinguishing Features:** man's body, goat's legs; sometimes given horns. **Supernatural Attributes:** immortality. **Page 5.**

Pan

PANDORA (pan-**door**-a) **Category:** demi-goddess. **Family Status:** created by Zeus; m. Epimetheus. **Career:** sent by Zeus to trick Epimetheus and punish mankind for accepting the gift of fire from Prometheus; she opened jar given her by Zeus, releasing all the evils into the world. **Personality:** incurably curious. **Supernatural Attributes:** immortality. **Page 21.**

PARIS (**pa**-riss) **Category:** human. **Family Status:** s. of Priam and Hecuba; lo. of Helen. **Career:** Trojan prince; destined to cause downfall of Troy – as predicted by the Oracle; he was abandoned to die as a baby, but survived; brought up by herdsman; chosen by Zeus to judge which was loveliest out of Hera, Athene and Aphrodite; chose Aphrodite and was promised the most beautiful woman in the world as his wife; offended Hera and Athene, which proved disastrous; as an adult, returned to Troy; his true identity was revealed and he was welcomed; went to Sparta on his father's business, saw Helen, fell in love and carried her off to Troy; Greeks stormed after to get her back, triggering start of the Trojan War; shot Achilles; was killed by archer, Philoctetes; Troy lost, so Paris did cause its ruin. **Personality:** rash and headstrong; susceptible to pretty women; sometimes said to be cowardly. **Supernatural Attributes:** had Aphrodite's protection but the disfavour of Hera and Athene working against him. **Distinguishing Features:** very good-looking. **Page 40.**

PATROCLUS (pat-**rock**-luss) **Category:** mortal. **Career:** Greek hero against the Trojans; great friend of Achilles; killed by Hector while impersonating Achilles to try and rally the discouraged Greeks. **Personality:** honourable; self-sacrificing. **Page 42.**

PEGASUS (peg-a-**suss**) **Category:** supernatural animal. **Family Status:** offspring of Poseidon and Medusa. **Career:** borrowed by hero, Bellerophon; helped him kill the Chimaera; took part in wars on behalf of King of Lycia; misused by Bellerophon in attempt to fly to Olympus; used by Zeus as instrument of Bellerophon's downfall; carries thunderbolts for Zeus. **Personality:** good-natured; obedient; neutrally loyal to any master – danger of being used to evil ends. **Distinguishing Features:** a horse with shining white coat; wings. **Supernatural Attributes:** flying ability.

Pegasus

PELEUS (**pee**-lyoos) **Category:** mortal. **Family Status:** m. Thetis; seven s., youngest was Achilles. **Career:** picked out by Zeus to marry the nereid, Thetis; had to catch her; found her and seized her; held on even while she changed shape and she eventually agreed to marry him; interrupted Thetis while making Achilles immortal, causing him to have one vulnerable spot – his heel. **Personality:** brave; persistent. **Page 23.**

PELIAS (**pee**-lee-ass) **Category:** mortal. **Family Status:** uncle to Jason; three d. **Career:** King of Iolcus after taking throne from Jason's father; sent Jason on quest for golden fleece, hoping he would not return; met violent death at the hands of his daughters, who were tricked by Medea into boiling him in a cauldron. **Personality:** ambitious; sly; sometimes underhand. **Pages 32, 33.**

PELOPS (**pell**-ops) **Category:** mortal. **Family Status:** s. of Tantalus; m. Hippodamia. **Career:** killed by his father and served to the gods at a feast; revived by gods and given ivory shoulder to replace one eaten by Demeter; helped by Poseidon to win chariot race for Hippodamia's hand against her father; renewed curse on his family by ingratitude to charioteer, Myrtilus, who also helped. **Personality:** daring, but egotistical; believes in taking what he wants; ungrateful. **Distinguishing Features:** ivory shoulder. **Supernatural Attributes:** favour of the gods after his mistreatment by his father. **Page 49**

PENELOPE (pen-**ell**-oh-pee) **Category:** mortal. **Family Status:** m. Odysseus; one s. Telemachus. **Career:** unhappily for her, Odysseus was away for twenty years, at the Trojan War and sailing home afterwards so she coped alone; was pressured by nobles to marry one of them; avoided this by saying she had to finish a piece of weaving first – she wove all day and then unpicked it at night so it was never finished; the trick was uncovered, and she was about to give in, when Odysseus returned; another short period of happiness followed, before Odysseus's death. **Personality:** loving wife and mother; famed for her fidelity; ingenious. **Pages 46, 47.**

PENTHEUS (pen-**thyoos**) **Category:** mortal. **Family Status:** s. of Agave. **Career:** King of Thebes; foolishly attempted to prevent his mother worshipping Dionysus because he disapproved; imprisoned Dionysus and was persuaded to go and watch Agave and the Maenads perform their rites; the women saw him and tore him apart – his mother ripped his head off. **Personality:** domineering – especially over women; foolish enough to oppose the gods. **Page 19.**

PERSEPHONE (per-**seff**-on-nee) **Roman:** Proserpina. **Category:** goddess. **Family Status:** d. of Zeus and Demeter; m. Pluto; lo. of Adonis. **Career:** helped her mother care for harvests and growing things until Pluto grabbed her to be his bride; very unhappy in Underworld; eventually found by Demeter, but could not leave Underworld permanently because she had eaten pomegranate seeds from Pluto's garden; special dispensation from Zeus to spend half the year with Pluto and half with Demeter; living things die in sorrow when she is away – the winter season; argued with Aphrodite over Adonis, leading to his death. **Personality:** rather sad and severe when in the Underworld; gay and happy when with Demeter. **Distinguishing Features:** represents spring and new growth. **Supernatural Attributes:** immortality. **Page 11.**

PERSEUS (per-**syoos**) **Category:** mortal. **Family Status:** s. of Zeus and Danae; m. Andromeda. **Career:** set afloat with his mother, because of prediction that he would kill his grandfather; cared for by King Polydictes on Seriphos; challenged by Polydictes to kill Medusa, the Gorgon, and succeeded with the help of the gods; saved Andromeda from a sea-monster and married her; prophesy came true when he accidentally killed his grandfather in a discus-throwing contest. **Personality:** protective of his mother; keen for adventure; bold and brave. **Supernatural Attributes:** was lent magic reflective shield, Hermes's winged sandals, Pluto's helmet of invisibility and a sickle by the gods. **Page 24.**

PHAEDRA (**feed**-ra) **Category:** mortal. **Family Status:** d. of Minos and Pasiphae; sister of Ariadne; m. Theseus. **Career:** second wife to Theseus; meanly claimed her step-son, Hippolytus, had attacked her, causing Theseus to ask Poseidon to punish him; Hippolytus was killed, Theseus found out he was innocent and Phaedra hanged herself for fear of the consequences. **Personality:** jealous; unscrupulous. **Page 25.**

PHAETHON (**feeth**-on) **Category:** god. **Family Status:** s. of Helios. **Career:** probably would have taken over chariot of the sun from his father when mature, but insisted on having a go at the reins while inexperienced; he lost control and had to

60

be struck down by Zeus to save the Earth; created Sahara Desert where he burned the Earth; mourned by his special friend, Cycnus. *Personality:* boastful; overconfident. **Page 26.**

PHILOCTETES (fill-**lock**-tee-teez) *Category:* mortal. *Career:* friend of Heracles; famous archer, he was given Heracles's bow when Heracles was taken to Olympus; set off for Troy with the Greeks; received snake bite on the way – wound would not heal so he was left behind; after death of Achilles, Odysseus came back begging for his help; he refused until visited in a dream by Heracles, telling him he would be healed if he helped; went to Troy and gave new hope to the troops; killed Paris; Greeks went on to win the war. *Personality:* proud; easily offended. **Page 43.**

PHINEUS (**fin**-ee-us) *Category:* mortal. *Career:* blind king and seer; life made a misery by the Harpies; visited by Jason and Argonauts; they drove the Harpies off in return for his help in getting past the Clashing Rocks. *Personality:* wise, shrewd. *Supernatural Attributes:* seeing the future. **Page 32.**

PHORCYS (**for**-sis) *Category:* god. *Family Status:* four d. Gorgons and Scylla. *Career:* sea-god; daughters turned into monsters by Athene. *Supernatural Attributes:* immortality. **Page 15.**

PHRIXUS (**fricks**-us) *Category:* mortal. *Family Status:* s. of Athamas and Nephele. *Career:* escaped sacrifice planned by his step-mother, Ino, on a golden ram sent by Hera; flew on ram's back to Colchis where he sacrificed it to Zeus; its fleece was hung in a sacred grove and guarded by a dragon serpent; Jason later went in search of the fleece. *Personality:* noble; respectful. **Page 25.**

PHYLLIS (**fill**-iss) *Category:* mortal. *Family Status:* due to m. Acamas. *Career:* waited for Acamas after he went to Trojan War; pined until she was about to die; Athene took pity and turned her into an almond tree; when Acamas retured he kissed the trunk of the tree and it blossomed, although the leaves were not yet out; the almond has flowered before its leaves appear ever since. *Personality:* faithful; sad. *Distinguishing Features:* took shape of an almond tree after her transformation. **Page 30.**

PINDAR Real person who wrote about the myths. He lived from 518-438 BC.

PIRITHOUS (pier-**rith**-o-us) *Category:* mortal. *Family Status:* s. of Ixion. King of Lapiths. *Career:* great friend and companion of Theseus; led him into scrapes; attempt to kidnap Persephone from Underworld ended in them being tied in chains of forgetfulness; left behind when Theseus rescued by Heracles. *Personality:* reckless to the point of foolishness; headstrong; bad influence. **Page 37.**

PLUTO (**ploo**-toe) *Roman:* Dis Pater. *Category:* god. *Family Status:* s. of Cronos and Rhea; m. Persephone. *Career:* swal-

lowed by his father at birth; rescued by Zeus; helped fight and defeat Cronos; given the Underworld as his kingdom; kidnapped Persephone against her will and married her. *Personality:* gloomy and frightening. *Distinguishing Features:* extremely rich - owns all precious metals and jewels. *Supernatural Attributes:* immortality; helmet of invisiblity that can be lent to mortals. *Associations:* planet named after him. **Pages 9, 10, 11, 27.**

POLYDEUCES (poll-ee-**dyoo**-seez) *Roman:* Pollux. *Category:* demi-god. *Family Status:* s. of Zeus and Leda; twin to Castor. *Career:* see **CASTOR.** *Personality:* heroic; strong family ties. *Supernatural Attributes:* immortality.

POLYDICTES (poll-ee-**dick**-teez) *Category:* mortal. *Family Status:* wanted to m. Danae. *Career:* King of Seriphos; rescued Danae and Perseus from the sea and looked after them; wished to marry Danae but was hindered by Perseus so suggested he attempt to kill Medusa; was about to force Danae to marry him when Perseus returned, with Medusa's head; Perseus took the head out and showed it to him and his courtiers and they turned to stone. *Personality:* generous; somewhat insensitive to the feelings of others. **Page 24.**

POLYPHEMUS (poll-ee-**fee**-muss) *Category:* Cyclops. *Family Status:* s. of Poseidon; descendent of the Cyclopes. *Career:* lived on Sicily; reared sheep to eat; captured Odysseus when he visited; blinded by Odysseus, who then escaped; called on Poseidon to curse Odysseus. *Personality:* dour; unfriendly; not sympathetic to humans. *Distinguishing Features:* giant stature; only one eye in the middle of his forehead. *Supernatural Attributes:* great strength. **Page 46.**

POSEIDON (poss-**eye**-don) *Roman:* Neptune. *Category:* god. *Family Status:* s. of Cronos and Rhea; m. Amphitrite; one s. Polyphemus (mo. possibly a Cyclops); sometimes said to be fa. of Bellerophon. *Career:* swallowed by his father at birth; rescued by Zeus; fought with Zeus against the Titans; given the Ocean as his kingdom; controlled storms and sea-monsters – drove Odysseus off-course, sent monster to devour Andromeda and a great wave to kill Hippolytus. *Personality:* less sociable than most other gods; does not mix with mortals much; powerful vengeance if angered. *Distinguishing Features:* three-pronged fork or Triton, made by Hephaestos. *Supernatural Attributes:* immortality; controlling the waves; causing earthquakes. *Associations:* called Earth-Shaker – Greeks assumed he made the Earth move in the same way he made the sea move. **Page 11.**

PRIAM (**pry**-am) *Category:* mortal. *Family Status:* m. many children incl. Hecuba; two s. Hector, Paris; one d. Cassandra. *Career:* King of Troy; sent Paris to Sparta to negotiate release of his sister, Hesione, who was their prisoner; lost Troy and was killed in the Trojan War. *Personality:* power-seeking; competitive, especially with Greeks.

PROMETHEUS (prom-**ee**-thee-us) *Category:* Titan. *Family Status:* s. of Uranus and Mother Earth; m. Hesione; one s. Deucalion. *Career:* fought with Zeus against Cronos; tutor to Athene; was asked to create a race to live on Earth by Zeus; created humans; tricked Zeus into accepting the worst part of a sacrifice, so mortals could have the good part; defied Zeus to give fire to mankind; was punished by a terrible torture – he was chained to a rock and an eagle was sent to tear out his liver; his liver was renewed every day and torn out again and again; eventually rescued by Heracles. *Personality:* great strength of character; wise, thoughtful. *Supernatural Attributes:* immortality. **Pages 20, 21.**

PROTEUS (**pro**-tee-us) see **BELLER-OPHON.**

PSYCHE (**sye**-kee) *Category:* mortal, becoming goddess. *Family Status:* m. Eros. *Career:* lived happily with her sisters until carried off by Eros, who visited her secretly; urged by her sisters, she lit a lamp to see who her lo. was; Eros disappeared and was forbidden to return by Aphrodite; she tried to appease Aphrodite by performing impossible tasks – helped each time by Eros; at last Zeus took pity, calmed Aphrodite and made Psyche immortal so she could marry Eros. *Personality:* easily influenced; vain; tenderhearted. *Distinguishing Features:* very beautiful; butterfly wings. *Supernatural Attributes:* immortality. *Associations:* "psyche" means "breath" and was used to refer to the non-physical part of a person – the mind or spirit; so "psychology" is the study of the human mind. **Page 31.**

PYGMALION (pig-**mail**-ee-on) *Category:* mortal. *Family Status:* m. Galatea. *Career:* sculptor; worshipper of Aphrodite; could not find true love so made statue of his ideal woman; he fell in love with the statue – rescued by Aphrodite who brought the statue to life so they could marry. *Personality:* artistic; determined; idealistic. *Distinguishing Features:* usually found with his sculptor's tools. *Associations:* George Bernard Shaw wrote a play called "Pygmalion", about a man who tried to mould a girl into his perfect woman. **Page 13.**

PYLADES (**pie**-lad-eez) *Category:* mortal. *Family Status:* cousin to Orestes; m. Electra. *Career:* accompanied Orestes to land of Taurians. *Personality:* brave; good friend. **Pages 44, 45.**

PYRRHA (**pir**-ra) *Category:* mortal. *Family Status:* d. of Epimetheus; m. Deucalion; ancestor of all mortal women. *Career:* see **DEUCALION.** *Personality:* worthy survivor. **Page 21.**

PYTHON (**pie**-thon) *Category:* monster. *Family Status:* Hera's servant. *Career:* obeyed Hera; was set on Leto, when Hera found out about her affair with Zeus; killed at Delphi by Apollo. *Personality:* vindictive. *Supernatural Attributes:* it was a gigantic snake. *Associations:* priestess of Apollo at Delphi called Pytheness. **Page 16.**

RHEA (**ree**-a) *Category:* Titaness. *Family Status:* d. of Uranus and Mother Earth; m. her brother, Cronos; three s. Zeus, Poseidon, Pluto; three d. Hestia, Demeter, Hera. *Career:* Queen of the Titans; unhappy marriage with Cronos because he swallowed all her children, due to prophesy that one of them would depose him; she saved Zeus, who rescued the rest of them; always shown great respect after Zeus and the New Gods took over. *Personality:* strong-willed; clever. *Supernatural Attributes:* immortality. **Page 8.**

SATYRS (**sat**-ires) *Category:* demigods. *Career:* spirits of nature; worshipping Dionysus; drinking and chasing nymphs. *Personalities:* mischievous troublemakers; extremely amorous. *Distinguishing Features:*

Satyr

young, handsome men with ears and tail of a horse. **Page 18.**

SCYLLA (**sill**-a) *Category:* mortal. *Family Status:* d. of King Nisus of Megara. *Career:* trapped in Megara while under siege by Minos; fell in love with Minos from the ramparts; wanted him to win the battle, so stole her father's magic lock of hair and took it to him; he accepted it but rejected Scylla for her treacherous behaviour; tried to swim after Minos but attacked by her father's spirit in the form of an eagle and drowned. *Personality:* romantic to a foolish degree; thoughtless. **Page 25.**

SCYLLA *Category:* monster. *Family Status: Career:* d. of Phorcys; loved by Poseidon; turned into a monster by jealous Amphitrite, killing sailors and wrecking ships; Odysseus was one of the few that escaped.

Scylla

Personality: deliberately evil; anti-mortals; noisy and terrifying. *Distinguishing Features:* female; six heads; ring of snarling dogs round her waist; always found in the vicinity of Charybdis, the whirlpool. *Supernatural Attributes:* enormous capacity to harm mortals. **Page 47.**

SEASONS (**see**-zunz) *Category:* demigoddesses. *Career:* gatekeepers of Olympus; often attended goddesses; brought clothes and jewels to Aphrodite when she was brought to Cyprus. *Distinguishing Features:* three of them – Spring, Summer and Winter. *Supernatural Attributes:* immortality. **Page 12.**

SELENE (sell-**ee**-nee) *Category:* Titaness. *Family Status:* d. of Hyperion and Theia. *Career:* drove chariot of the moon; often confused with Artemis; was loved by Endymion, who was put in eternal sleep by Zeus so he could dream about her. *Personality:* distant; unapproachable. *Supernatural Attributes:* immortality.

SEMELE (**sem**-a-lee) *Category:* mortal. *Family Status:* d. of Cadmus; lo. of Zeus; one s. Dionysus (fa. Zeus). *Career:* while expecting Zeus's child, Hera persuaded her to insist on seeing his true form; struck dead when he appeared as lightning and blasted her; their son, Dionysus, was saved by Zeus and he took his mo. to Olympus. *Personality:* inquisitive; gullible. **Page 18.**

SILENUS (sye-**leen**-us) *Category:* demigod; satyr. *Career:* worshipping Dionysus; indulging himself in a good time; it was for looking after him when in a drunken stupor that Dionysus granted Midas a wish *Personality:* pleasure-seeking; irresponsible. *Distinguishing Features:* fat and old; often drunk; frequently seen riding an ass. **Page 18.**

SILVER RACE *Category:* mortal. *Family Status:* created by Zeus. *Career:* unsuccessful race made by Zeus to live on Earth to replace the Golden Race; turned out to be evil so were all destroyed by Zeus. *Personalities:* wilfully [1] d. **Page 20.**

SIRENS (**sye**-runs) *Category:* monsters. *Career:* singing to lure sailors onto the jagged rocks where they lived and wrecking their ships; only Jason and Odysseus ever managed to escape – Odysseus actually heard their singing without dying by hav-

Siren

ing himself tied to the mast. *Personalities:* destructive; wicked. *Distinguishing Features:* very beautiful female faces and voices; bird-like bodies with wings and claws. *Supernatural Attributes:* their voices, which are irresistibly attractive to humans. **Pages 33, 47.**

SISYPHUS (**sis**-ee-fuss) *Category:* mortal. *Family Status:* s. of Aeolus. *Career:* was a friend of Zeus but betrayed secrets told him by the god; stole his brother's throne; seduced his niece; Zeus sent Pluto to take him to Tartarus; he tricked Pluto into trying on his own chains and made him prisoner, causing havoc, as no-one could die without Pluto to guide them to the Underworld; Ares was sent to rescue Pluto; Sisyphus was punished by being made to roll a boulder up a steep hill in Tartarus – each time he got to the top it rolled back down again so he could never complete his task. *Personality:* cunning; egotistical; ungrateful. **Page 27.**

SOPHOCLES (**soff**-oh-kleez) Real man. Wrote plays about the myths.

SOUTH WIND see **AUSTER.**

SPHINX (**sfincks**) *Category:* monster. *Family Status:* child of Orthrus and Echidne. *Career:* challenging humans to answer her riddle (see page 29) and killing them if they cannot; cor-

Sphinx

rect answer was "a man" – he crawls on all-fours when a weak baby, walks on his two legs when a strong youth and uses a stick as a third leg when feeble and old; given the correct answer by Oedipus; committed suicide in shame. *Personality:* evil; smug. *Distinguishing Features:* woman's head, lion's body, wings; to be found on the road to Thebes. *Associations:* Sphinxes feature in Egyptian myths, too, **Page 29.**

STYMPHALIAN BIRDS (stim-**fail**-ee-an birds) *Category:* monsters. *Career:* scavenging and disturbing the people of Stymphalus because of their great numbers. *Personalities:* greedy nuisances. *Distinguishing Features:* birds with bronze beaks, wings and claws. **Page 38.**

TALOS (**ta**-los) *Category:* monster. *Family Status:* servant to Minos. *Career:* made by Hephaestos; threw boulders to ward off strangers approaching Crete; killed when Medea took out the pin that held his life force in his body. *Distinguishing Features:* giant made of bronze; to be found striding round Crete. *Supernatural Attributes:* giant strength. **Page 33.**

TANTALUS (**tan**-ta-luss) *Category:* mortal. *Family Status:* s. of Zeus and a Titaness; two s. incl. Pelops; one d. Niobe. *Career:* initially great friend of the gods; ate ambrosia and nectar with them; invited them to a banquet where he dished up his son for them to eat, simply to see if they could tell what they were eating; he could not fool the gods and was punished in Tartarus by having food and drink placed near him but just out of reach; if he tried to stretch out for it, it moved away. *Personality:* consciously wicked; misused his privileged position. *Distinguishing Features:* eternally up to his neck in water in Tartarus. *Associations:* the word "tantalizing", used to describe something desirable but out of reach, comes from his name; **Page 27.**

TELEMACHUS (tell-e-**mack**-us) *Category:* mortal. *Family Status:* s. of Odysseus and Penelope. *Career:* grew up without his father, who was at Trojan War and then on his travels; protected his mother, but could not stop nobles bothering her and wasting his father's wealth; helped Odysseus once he returned and revealed who he was; stole the weapons of the nobles courting Penelope and helped kill them when they were defenceless. *Personality:* honorable and brave but inexperienced. **Pages 46, 47.**

THEMIS (**thee**-miss) *Category:* Titaness. *Family Status:* d. of Uranus and Mother Earth. *Career:* sent by Zeus to help Deucalion and Pyrrha found human race after the flood. *Supernatural Attributes:* immortality. **Page 21.**

THESEUS (**thee**-syoos) *Category:* mortal. *Family Status:* s. of Aegeus and Aethra; lo. of Ariadne; m. Hippolyte; m. Phaedra; one s. Hipplytus (mo. Hippolyte). *Career:* volunteered to go to Crete as one of the victims of the Minotaur; Ariadne fell in love with him and helped him; he killed the Minotaur and escaped with the other victims and Ariadne; left Ariadne behind on the way home, on Naxos; forgot to change the sails from black to white to herald the news that he was safe, causing his father to commit suicide in despair; became king and m. Hippolyte, who was killed in battle; lost his son due to wicked plots of second wife, Phaedra; disillusioned, he took to adventuring; led on madcap scheme to kidnap Persephone by Pirithous; caught by the gods and tied in chains of forgetfulness; rescued by Heracles; lost his kingdom, retired to Scyros; his body brought back to Athens and buried with honour after his ghost appeared and spurred the troops to victory at the battle of Marathon. *Personality:* good, courageous and bold in his youth; became reckless adventurer after tragic loss of his son. *Supernatural Attributes:* his love of Athens lived on after his death and his ghost was often said to appear to soldiers defending the city. **Pages 34, 36.**

THETIS (**thee**-tiss) *Category:* demi-goddess; nereid. *Family Status:* lo. of Zeus; m. Peleus; seven s., incl. Achilles. *Career:* Zeus wanted to marry her but did not because it was predicted that any son she had would be greater than its father, a risk Zeus could not take; Zeus sent Peleus to catch and marry her; she tried to escape by assuming different shapes but gave in eventually; Eris brought apple inscribed "For the fairest" to their wedding – cause of Trojan War; made six of her sons immortal, but Achilles was left with one vulnerable spot on his heel because she was interrupted by Peleus. *Distinguishing Features:* normal shape is a beautiful woman. *Supernatural Attributes:* shape-changing ability. **Page 23.**

TIRESIAS (tire-**ee**-see-us) *Category:* mortal. *Family Status:* blinded by Athene; became great seer; found out Oedipus's true identity; gave Odysseus advice when visited by him in the Underworld. *Personality:* very knowledgeable; gives good advice. *Distinguishing Features:* an old man with a stick. *Supernatural Attributes:* telling the future. **Pages 29, 47.**

TITANS (**tie**-tans) *Family Status:* descendants of Uranus and Mother Earth. *Career:* were rulers of the world until revolt led by Zeus; after this, most of them were imprisoned in Tartarus; see **CRONOS, RHEA, PROMETHEUS, ATLAS.** *Personalities:* varied – some good, some bad. *Distinguishing Features:* giant size. *Supernatural Attributes:* immortality. **Page 8.**

TROS (**tross**) *Category:* mortal. *Family Status:* one s. Ganymede. *Career:* King of Troy, which was named after him.

TYNDAREUS (tin-**dar**-yoos) *Category:* mortal. *Family Status:* m. Leda; one s. Castor; one d. Clytemnestra. *Career:* king; cared for Leda's children by Zeus as well as his own offspring; chose Menelaus as husband for Helen; made Helen's suitors swear to support her husband. *Personality:* kind and generous; clever. **Page 41.**

URANUS (you-**rain**-us) *Category:* god. *Family Status:* s. of Mother Earth; m. Mother Earth; many children incl. giants, Cyclopes, Titans, Titanesses; fa. of Erinyes and Aphrodite. *Career:* he is the sky; he and Mother Earth produced all living things; he was displeased with some of them and imprisoned them in Tartarus; Mother Earth turned against him and encouraged Titans to rebel; defeated by Cronos with a sickle; where his blood fell on Earth, the Erinyes appeared; Aphrodite was born from the foam caused when his blood dropped in the ocean. *Personality:* heartless; cruel. *Supernatural Attributes:* fathering monstrous offspring; immortality. *Associations:* planet named after him. **Page 8.**

VENUS (**vee**-nuss) see **APHRODITE.**

WEST WIND see **ZEPHYR.**

ZEPHYR (**zeff**-er) *Category:* god. *Family Status:* under the control of Aeolus. *Career:* West Wind; blew mild, warm winds as directed. *Distinguishing Features:* young, handsome man, sometimes with a serpent's tail. *Supernatural Attributes:* flying with the wind.

ZEUS (**zyoos**) *Roman:* Jupiter. *Category:* god. *Family Status:* s. of Cronos and Rhea; m. his sister, Hera and had one s. Ares, two d. Eris, Hebe; one d., Athene, born from his head; lo. of Semele, Io, Europa, Danae, Leda, Alcmene and many others; sons incl. Perseus (mo. Danae), Heracles (mo. Alcmene), Tantalus (mo. Titaness), Polydictes (mo. Leda), Minos, Rhadamanthys, Sarpedon (mo. Europa); daughters incl. Helen (mo. Leda). *Career:* saved by his mother from being swallowed at birth by Cronos; grew up safely and staged a rebellion; released his brothers and sisters; defeated Cronos and took over as King of the gods; ruled from Olympus; very fond of visiting the Earth and getting involved in human affairs. *Personality:* dominating; powerful; soft spot for pretty women; terrifying when angry. *Distinguishing features:* thunderbolts made by Cyclopes to be hurled when annoyed. *Supernatural Attributes:* immortality; all-powerful to do what he wants with mortals - strike them down, turn them into animals, cause the defeat of an army etc. *Associations:* eagle was his bird; oaks sacred to him. **Pages 9, 11, 22, 23.**

Index

Acamas 30, 50
Achaea/ans 4, 48
Achaeus 48, 50
Achilles 42, 50
Acrisius 22, 24, 50
Acropolis 15
Actaeon 17, 48, 50
Adonis 13, 50
Aeaea 47
Aeetes 32, 33, 50
Aegean 4, 36
Aegeus 34, 36, 50
aegis 14
Aegisthus 44, 45, 50
Aegyptus 25, 50
Aeneas 13, 42, 44, 51
Aeolians 48
Aeolus 46, 48, 51
Aeschylus 5
Agamemnon 17, 41, 42, 44, 49, 51
Agave 19, 51
Age of Heroes 21
Ajax 43, 51
Alcmene 23, 51
Alexander the Great 7
almond tree 30
alphabet 19
Amazon 36, 38, 51
ambrosia 27
Amphitrite 11, 36, 51
Anchises 13, 42, 51

Andromeda 24, 51
anemone 13
Antigone 29, 48, 51
Aphrodite 12, 13, 31, 40, 41, 51
Apollo 5, 16, 17, 19, 26, 27, 29, 42, 45, 48, 49, 51
Aquarius 48, 51
Arachne 15, 51
Arcadia 4
Ares 12, 13, 27, 51
Argo/nauts 32, 33, 39, 51
Argos 4, 25, 28
Argus 22, 51
Ariadne 36, 52
Arion 49, 52
Aristaeus 48, 52
Artemis 16, 17, 29, 38, 42, 44, 45, 48, 52
Arts 16
Asclepius 17, 29, 52
Asphodel Fields 10,
Athamas 25, 52
Athene 14, 15, 21, 24, 28, 41, 43, 44, 45, 49, 52
Athens 4, 15, 30, 34, 36
Atlas 9, 39, 52
Attica 4
Augeas/ean 48, 52

Aulis 4
Auster 48, 52
Bacchae/us 52
barber 27
bear 17
bees 48
Bellerophon 52
Bible 5
boar 13
Boeotia 4
Boreas 30, 48, 52
box 21
boxing 19
bronze 33, 38
Bronze Race 20, 52
bulls 6, 22, 32, 34, 38
Cadmus 18, 49, 52
Calchas 49, 52
Callisto 17, 52
Calypso 47, 52
Cape Sounion 4
Capri 33
Cassandra 41, 44, 53
Castor 23, 53
cattle 19, 38, 47
centaur 53
Cerberus 39, 53
Ceres 53
Cerynean hind 38, 53
Ceuta 38
Chaos 8,
Charon 11, 53

Charybdis 47, 53
chariot 13, 16, 17, 25, 26, 49
Chimaera 28, 53
Circe 47, 53
Clashing Rocks 32, 53
cloud-woman 25, 26
Clytemnestra 23, 44, 45, 53
Colchis 25, 32
Corinth 4, 29, 33
costume 3
cow 19, 22
crafts 15
Creation 8
Creon 48, 53
Crete 4, 6, 22, 25, 26, 33, 34, 36
Cronos 8, 9, 20, 53
Cyclopes 8, 9, 17, 46, 53
Cyprus 12
Cyrene 48
Cythera 4, 12
Daedalus 26, 34, 49, 53
Danae 22, 24, 54
Danaus 25, 54
Daphne 16, 54
Deianeira 39, 54
Delos 4, 16, 29
Delphi/ic 4, 5, 16, 25, 45

Demeter 11, 31, 49, 54
Deucalion 21, 48, 54
Diana 54
Dido 54
Diomedes 38, 54
Dionysus 18, 19, 27, 31, 36, 54
discus 24, 48
disguise 23
doctor 17
dog 38, 39
dolphin 49
Dorians 48
Dorus 48, 54
drama 5
dragon-serpent 33
dragon's teeth 32
dryads 54
eagle 21, 25, 29, 39, 48
Earth 8, 10, 11, 20, 21, 23, 26, 27, 48,
East Wind 48, 54
Echidne 54
Echo 30, 54
Egypt 22
Electra 44, 45, 54
Elysian Fields 10,
Endymion 17, 54
Eos 29, 54
Epimetheus 21, 54
Erinyes 8, 54
Eris 23, 40, 55

Eros 13, 31, 55
Erymanthian boar 38
Eumenides 55
Euripides 5, 55
Europa 22, 49, 55
Eurus 48, 55
Eurydice 31, 48, 55
Eurystheus 37, 38, 39, 55
Evans, Sir Arthur 34
fantasy gamers 2
Fate 28, 29, 31, 36
festivals 5
fire 20, 21, 23, 25
flood 21
flute 14, 17
foam 12
forethought 20
forge 12, 21
frenzy 19
Furies 8, 28, 45, 55
Galatea 13, 55
Ganymede 48, 55
Games 24, 41
Geryon 38, 55
giant 8, 33, 46
Gibraltar 38
Glaucis 33, 55
Glaucus 13, 55
goddess of love 12
    of wisdom 14
    of spite 23, 40
    virgin- 14
god messenger- 19
    of the Arts 16
    smith- 12
    sun- 5, 16
gods combining 3
    Olympian 18
gold 8, 22, 27, 38
golden apples 39
    fleece 32
Golden Race 20, 55
Gorgons 15, 24, 55
grapes 18
Great Bear 17
Greece-Ancient 5
    Archaic 7
    Classical 7
    Dark Ages 7
    Hellenistic 7
gymnastics 19
Hades 10, 11, 27, 55,
Haemon 48, 55
hair 25
Harmonia 13, 55
Harpies 32, 55
Hebe 48, 55
Hector 42, 55
Hecuba 40, 56
Helen 23, 36, 40, 41, 43, 45, 56
Helios 26, 56
Helle 25, 56
Hellen/enes 48, 56
Hellespont 4, 25, 40
helmet 9, 24
    winged 19
Hephaestos 12, 14, 21, 56
Hera 9, 11, 16, 18, 22, 23, 25, 26, 30, 37, 39, 40, 41, 56
Heracles 23, 37, 38, 39, 43, 56

Hercules 37
Hermes 19, 22, 24, 26, 41, 47, 56
Hermione 45, 56
hero/oes 2, 10, 22, 28, 32, 33, 34, 37, 42, 48
Hesione 41, 56
Hesperides 39, 56
Hestia 9, 56
Hippodamia 49, 56
Hippolyte 36, 38, 56
Hippolytus 25, 36, 56
history 5
Hittites 40
Homer 7, 40, 46, 57
Hope 14
horses 13, 25, 43
hounds 17, 48
hunting 16, 17
Hyacinthus 48, 57
Hyperion 47, 57
Icaria 4, 26
Icarian Sea 4
Icarus 26, 57
Iliad 7
immortal/s 21, 31, 42
Immortal/s 12, 14, 29, 37, 39, 48
Io 22, 57
Iolcus 4, 32, 33
Ion/ians 48, 57
Iphigenia 17, 41, 44, 45, 57
Iris 57
Isis 22
Isles of the Blessed 10,
Italy 44
Ithaca 4, 46, 47
Ixion 26, 57
jar 21, 25, 31
Jason 6, 32-33, 34, 57
Jocasta 29, 57
Julius Caesar 44
Knossos 4, 34
Koran 5
Labyrinth 34, 36
Laius 29, 57
laurel 16
Leda 23, 41, 57
legend 2, 6, 7, 49
Lerna 4
Lernaean Hydra 37, 57
Lesbos 4
Leto 16, 42, 57
liars 19
Libya 46
lion 23, 28, 29, 37
Lion Gate 6
liver 21
Lotus-Eaters 46, 57
love 12, 22, 23, 30, 40
Lycia 28
Lyra 31
lyre 7, 16, 17, 19, 31, 33
Macedonia 4
Maenads 31, 19, 57
Maia 19, 58
Marathon 4, 36
Marsyas 15, 17, 58
maze 34, 36
Mediterranean 7, 38
Medea 32, 33, 34, 39, 58
Medusa 15, 24, 58

Megara 25, 37, 58
Menelaus 41, 43, 45, 46, 58
Metis 14, 58
Midas 27, 58
Minerva 58
Minoans 6, 34
Minos 6, 22, 25, 26, 33, 34, 36, 49, 58
Minotaur 34, 36, 38, 58
monster 2, 8, 10, 15, 24, 29, 33
moon 16, 17
Mopsus 49, 58
Morocco 38
mortal 20, 23, 29
Mother Earth 8, 16, 29, 58
Mount Erymanthos 4
Mount Ida 4
Mount Olympus 4, 11, 31, 39,
Mount Parnassus 4, 21
Mount Sipylus 16
murderer/ess 44
Muses 16, 58
music/ician 16, 19, 31, 49
Mycenae/aeans 4, 6, 44
Myrtilus 49, 58
mystery cults 5, 19
naiads 58
Narcissus 30, 58
Naxos 4, 36
nectar 27
Nemea 4
Nemean Lion 37
Nemesis 59
Neoptolemus 43, 59
Nephele 25, 26, 59
nereid 11, 23, 24, 36, 59
New Gods 12, 20, 59
Niobe 16, 59
Nisus 25, 59
North Wind 48, 59
nymphs 8, 11, 16, 17, 18, 24, 30, 33, 48, 49, 59
obol 11
Ocean 9, 11, 63
Odysseus 41, 43, 46, 47, 59
Odyssey 7, 46
Oedipus 29, 48, 59
Oenomaus 49
olive 14, 15
Olympia 4
Olympus 11, 28, 45, 48,
Oracles 5, 16, 22, 24, 25, 29, 37, 44, 45, 59
Oreithyia 30, 59
Orestes 44, 45, 49, 59
Orion 29, 59
Orpheus 31, 33, 48, 59
Orthrus 38, 60
Ortygia 16, 47
owl 14
Pallas 14, 60
Palladium 44
Pan 5, 60
Pandora 21, 60
Paris 40-43, 44, 60
Parthenon/os 15
Pasiphae 60
Patroclus 42, 60

patron/ess 19
Pegasus 28, 60
Peleus 23, 40, 42, 60
Pelias 32, 33, 60
Pelops 27, 49, 60
Penelope 46, 47, 60
Pentheus 19, 60
Persephone 11, 13, 31, 36, 60
Perseus 22, 24, 60
Persians 30
Phaedra 25, 36, 60
Phaethon 26, 60
Philoctetes 43, 61
Phineus 32, 61
Phorcys 15, 61
Phrixus 25, 32, 61
Phyllis 30, 61
pigs 47
Pillars of Heracles 38
Pindar 61
Pirithous 36, 61
plays 5, 7
Pluto 9, 10, 11, 17, 24, 27, 31, 39, 61
poet/poetry 7, 49
poison 34, 39
Polydeuces 23, 61
Polydictes 24, 61
Polyphemus 46, 61
pomegranate 11
Poseidon 5, 9, 11, 15, 24, 25, 34, 36, 46, 49, 61
Priam 40, 41, 42, 61
princess 15, 18, 30, 41
Prometheus 20, 21, 48, 61
pronounciation 3
Proteus 28, 61
Psyche 31
punishment 21, 26
Pygmalion 13, 61
Pylades 45, 61
Python/ess 5, 16, 61
Pyrrha 21, 61
raven 16
reeds 27
retribution 44, 45
revenge 19, 36, 37, 41
Rhea 8, 18, 62
riddle 29
Rome/Roman 7, 37, 44
Sardinia 48
satyrs 17, 18, 19, 62
scallop 12
Schliemann, Heinrich 6, 40
Scorpio/on 29
Scylla 25, 47, 62
Scyros 4, 36
Seasons 12, 62
seer 47, 49
Selene 17, 62
Semele 18, 62
Seriphos 4, 22, 24
serpent 23, 29, 37, 49
shades 10
Sicily 47, 48
Silenus 18, 19, 27, 62
Silver Race 20, 62
sirens 33, 47, 62
Sisyphus 27, 28, 62
Sleep of Death 31

snakes 24, 30, 42, 48
Sophocles 5, 62
South Wind 16, 48, 62
Spain 38
Sparta/n 4, 6, 23, 41, 45, 48
Sphinx 29, 62
spider 15
spite 23, 40
stags 16, 17
stars 48
statue 13, 45
Straits of Bosphorous 32
Stymphalian birds 38, 62
Stymphalos 4
Styx 11,
suitors 41
sun 5, 16
swan 23
Talos 33, 62
Tantalus 27, 44, 49, 62
Tartarus 10, 17, 20, 25, 27, 36, 39,
Taurians 45
Telemachus 41, 46, 47, 62
Thebes 16, 18, 19, 29, 48
Themis 21, 63
Theseus 25, 34, 36, 62
Thetis 36, 42, 47, 63
thief 19
Thrace 4, 48
thunder/bolts 9, 18, 26
thyrsos 19
Tiresias 15, 29, 47, 63
Titaness 14, 16, 17, 18, 19, 21
Titan 8, 9, 18, 20, 39, 47, 63
trick 20, 23, 43, 46
trident 9, 15
Trojan War 23, 42, 44
    Horse 43
Tros 48, 63
Troy 4, 17, 36, 40, 41, 42, 44, 46, 48
Turkey 40
Twelve Labours 37, 38
Tyndareus 23, 63
Tyre 22
Underworld 8, 9, 10, 11, 13, 24, 31, 39, 47,
Uranus 8, 12, 63
Venus 44, 63
West Wind 48, 63
Who's Who 50-63
wind 24, 27, 41, 46
wine 18
winged helmet 19
    horse 28
    sandals 19, 24
wings 26
Zephyr 48, 63
Zeus 8, 9, 10, 11, 12, 13, 14, 16, 17, 18, 19, 20, 21, 22, 23, 26, 27, 28, 29, 30, 31, 37, 44, 45, 47, 48, 63